CW00969861

The
Ultimate Reading FC
Quiz Book

Jon Keen

MICKLE PRESS

First Published in paperback in Great Britain in June 2020 by Mickle Press.

A CIP catalogue record for this book is available from the British Library.

ISBN: 978-0-9935175-2-5

MICKLE PRESS

www.micklepress.com

Author's Note

I first thought of writing a Reading FC quiz book shortly after I had finished writing "*The Sum of the Parts*" as something to help Loyal Royals pass the time on long trips to away matches. By the time I sat down and started writing it, in April 2020, the 2019/20 football season had been suspended due to the Covid-19 lockdown, and at the time of publication it's still not clear when supporters will next be able to attend away matches. But I hope this won't stop everyone enjoying the 150 quizzes I've put together.

The answers in this book are believed to be correct as at 1st June 2020. I've checked everything as diligently I can, and I've received invaluable assistance in proof-reading and fact-checking from Dave Harris, Fiona Keen and Ian McLean. My thanks to them, plus even greater thanks to Andrew Bryant, Nigel Meek and Chris Straw who have donated hours of their time going through the text with an eye to detail I can't ever hope to match. Without their efforts this book would be far less trustworthy!

Having said that, in any book with 1,500 questions it's inevitable that there are some errors which have been missed by all of us – for these, I can only apologise and assure you that we have done everything possible to eliminate them.

Numerous sources have been used in preparing this book, foremost amongst them Alan Sedunary's excellent "*Heaven on Earth – The Official History of Reading FC 1871 -2003*" and "*The Definitive Reading FC*" by David Downs and Leigh Edwards. However, football and journalism being what they are, some sources differ between each other on some facts - especially things like attendances, goal times and transfer fees etc. – and the further back you go the more likely you are to find such differences. Again, my apologies if this makes your answer to a question a wrong answer!

Thanks for purchasing this book, and I hope you enjoy it. My personal recommendation would be that you treat it like a swimming pool – dip into it at regular intervals, and come up feeling exhilarated and in need of a strong drink!

Contents

Questions

Quiz 1 – Origins *(Answers on page 102)*

1   Where was the meeting to found Reading Football Club held?
2   Who was Reading's founder and first chairman?
3   On what date did Reading play their first game?
4   Where was this match played, and who were the opposition?
5   What was the most likely formation Reading lined up in during their first games?
6   Where was Reading's first game outside Reading played?
7   Who scored Reading's first ever goal?
8   Why did Reading's match away at Maidenhead in March 1873 end after 70 minutes?
9   Reading took on several players from another local team that folded in March 1876 having suffered a 10-0 defeat. Which team?
10   In which competition was Reading's first competitive match, in November 1877?

Quiz 2 – Transfer Trails (1) *(Answers on page 102)*

Name the Reading player from their transfer history. The number of league appearances made for Reading is shown in brackets.

11   Spurs > Watford (loan) > Reading (202) > Notts County > Bristol City > Hornchurch > Peterborough
12   Reading (42) > Shrewsbury Town (loan) > Crewe Alexandra (loan) > 1899 Hoffenheim > Swansea City (loan) > Spurs > Swansea City > Everton
13   Stratford Town > Charlton Athletic > Reading (500) > Birmingham City > Newbury Town
14   Leyton Orient > Reading (267) > Aston Villa > Nottingham Forest (loan) > Fulham (loan) > West Bromwich Albion > Reading (17) > Bristol City > Portsmouth > Pune City > Colchester United
15   West Ham > Reading (471)

16   Torres > Reading (209) > Maidenhead United (loan) >
      Northwood (loan) > Carshalton Athletic (loan) > Southend
      (loan) > AFC Bournemouth > Stoke City

17   Leicester City > Bradford (loan) > Brentford (loan x 2) >
      Bristol City (loan) > Reading (160)

18   Hayes > Reading (121) > Cardiff City

19   Reading (262) > Wimbledon > Swindon Town > Sligo
      Rangers

20   Walsall > Cambridge United > Reading (103) > Rotherham
      > Walsall > Grimsby Town > Burton Albion

Quiz 3 – Reading & Arsenal *(Answers on page 102)*

21   Which Arsenal player was retrospectively suspended after
      video evidence showed him slap Graeme Murty off the ball?

22   What was unusual about the two Arsenal goals that knocked
      Reading out of the FA Cup in February 1972?

23   Which Arsenal player scored a hat-trick in the unbelievable 7-
      5 League Cup win over the Royals in October 2012?

24   Which best-selling book includes a chapter about the author
      supporting Arsenal at Elm Park in 1972?

25   What was the score in Reading's first ever Football League
      match vs. Arsenal?

26   Which defender, who won three Premier League titles with
      Arsenal, joined Reading for just four months before retiring?

27   Whose goalkeeping error gifted Arsenal their passage to the
      FA Cup final at Reading's expense?

28   In Highbury's final season, which ex-Arsenal goalkeeper
      started in goal for Reading in their League Cup match there?

29   What is the family relationship between former Arsenal and
      England coach Don Howe and Reading's CEO Nigel Howe?

30   Who scored Reading's only goal against Arsenal in the 3-1 FA
      Cup 3rd Round defeat at Elm Park in January 1987?

Quiz 4 –Southern League Years *(Answers on page 103)*

31   Which perennial local rival team did Reading beat 4-3 away in
      their first Southern League match in September 1894?

32   What major change of status did Reading finally make at a meeting in May 1895 in order to ensure they could compete in the Southern League?

33   What position did Reading finish in their only ever season in the Southern League Second Division, after being relegated from the First Division in 1909/10?

34   Who was Reading's first professional captain, signed from Middlesbrough in 1895?

35   What was Reading's highest ever finish in the Southern League First Division?

36   By what convincing margin did Reading win an away FA Cup tie at Wycombe Wanderers in October 1899?

37   Which team, later to win seven European Cups, did Reading beat 5-0 in 1913, leading to newspaper *Corriere della Sera* writing "without doubt, Reading FC are the finest foreign team seen in Italy"?

38   Name Reading's top scorer in the four seasons before World War I - he joined the "Footballers' Battalion" in 1915 and was killed at Delville Wood, on the Somme, in August 1916.

39   Which Yorkshire club, later members of the Football League until 1970, were Southern League opponents for a single season in 1907/08?

40   On Easter Monday 1918, what sport was played at Elm Park between a Canadian and a USA team?

Quiz 5 – Madejski Stadium (1) *(Answers on page 103)*

41   Who were Reading's first opponents at the Madejski Stadium?

42   Which rugby team ground-shared with Reading for two years from 1998?

43   How much did John Madejski pay Reading Borough Council to purchase the land for the new stadium?

44   Who scored the first competitive goal at the stadium?

45   Which Premier League team were the visitors in November 2012 when the stadium's attendance record of 24,184 was set?

46   What was the original name of the bar in the East Stand, now "The Jazz Café"?

47 In May 2007 plans to extend the MadStad were announced. What would have been the new capacity if these had gone through?

48 Which visiting team saw the MadStad's lowest ever league attendance, 5,393, in October 1999?

49 Which Californian rock band played a concert at the Madejski in July 2006?

50 Name the Reading player who scored two goals for England in their win over Germany in an Under-20 international at the Madejski in February 2003.

Quiz 6 – Reading & Aston Villa *(Answers on page 103)*

51 Which Villa player scored a hat-trick at the MadStad to knock Reading out of the FA Cup in March 2010?

52 Which Reading central defender was harshly sent off at Villa Park in Reading's first away Premier League match?

53 Which Ecuador international joined Reading from Villa in August 2006?

54 Whose 90th minute penalty rescued a point for Reading at Villa Park in August 2018?

55 Which Reading striker needed surgery to his face after a stamp by Tyrone Mings?

56 Which two members of the 106 point team played together at Villa in 2008/09?

57 Which player, now a TV presenter, scored the only goal as Reading lost 1-0 at Villa Park in the 2001/02 League Cup?

58 In the last match of 1970/71, Reading needed a draw at Villa Park to avoid relegation. What was the score in that game?

59 Which promising youngster joined Villa for a reported £5M after just 13 Reading league appearances?

60 Who scored both Reading goals in their home Premier League win over Villa in February 2007?

Quiz 7 – Reading in the 1920s *(Answers on page 104)*

61 Which of their star players did Reading sell to Sheffield Wednesday for £650 in 1920?

62 Who were the opponents in Reading's first Football League match at Elm Park?

63 Who scored 17 league goals in Reading's first season in the Football League, 1920/21?

64 To which off-field role was Arthur Chadwick appointed in January 1923?

65 Who became the first Reading player to be sent off in a Football League game, against Exeter in December 1922?

66 Which centre-half, signed from Notts. Forest in 1923, missed only six games between December 1923 and April 1930?

67 Reading played their last match of 1925/26, at home to Brentford, needing a win to have any chance of ensuring promotion to Division Two. What was the final score?

68 Who scored 12 goals in the final 13 games of 1925/26 to help Reading win Division Three (South)?

69 After a famously fractious home match, and a drawn replay at Old Trafford, where did Reading's 2-1 FA Cup 3rd Round win over Manchester United in January 1927 take place?

70 Who scored 19 goals from 28 games as Reading finished 15th in Division Two in 1928/29?

Quiz 8 – Play-offs (1) *(Answers on page 104)*

71 Which of Reading's four play-off finals was watched by the biggest crowd?

72 Who did Reading beat in the 1995 play-off semi-finals to reach Wembley?

73 Which Reading striker's head did the ball bounce off in his own area to gift Walsall a bizarre own goal in Cardiff in 2001?

74 And which Reading centre-back made the clearance that bounced off him into his own net?

75 Who scored first to give Royals a lead at Wolves in 2003?

76 Which three members of the 106 point squad came off the bench in the 52nd and 53rd minutes of the 2009 play-off semi-final at home to Burnley?

77 What did Reading fans hold in the air whilst celebrating their dominance at the City of Cardiff Stadium in the 2011 play-off semi-final?

78 Who refereed the 2017 play-off final?

79   Which local radio reporter promised to walk to Wembley if Reading made it there in 1995?

80   Which ex-Walsall player restored Reading's lead against his old club in 2001?

Quiz 9 – Reading & Brum/Coventry *(Answers on page 104)*

81   Which defender did Reading sign on a free transfer from Birmingham City in July 2019?

82   What was the score on Reading's first visit to the Ricoh Arena, in September 2005?

83   Who scored a hat-trick for Birmingham in their 6-1 win over Reading in December 2014?

84   And who scored Reading's one goal in that game?

85   At what time did the epic Simod Cup semi-final against Coventry at Elm Park in 1988 finally end?

86   Which Reading centre-back joined Coventry City on a free transfer in November 2004?

87   Which much-loved striker joined Reading from Birmingham for £650,000 in June 1999?

88   Who scored Reading's three goals in their win at St Andrews in the last match before the Covid-19 lockdown in 2020?

89   Which player, signed from Coventry in May 1938, scored 217 goals in 252 World War II matches?

90   Who scored two goals at St Andrews in January 2007 in a 3-2 Reading win in the 4th Round of the FA Cup?

Quiz 10 – Reading in the 1930s *(Answers on page 105)*

91   What long-serving organisation associated with the football club was formed in December 1930?

92   Who scored six goals for Reading in their 7-3 win over Stoke City in April 1931?

93   Which team finished two points ahead of Reading in Division Three (South) in 1931 to claim the top spot and only promotion place?

94   Reading's top scorer, with 29 goals from 27 games, was sold to Stoke for £2,500 in March 1933. Name him.

95   Who scored on his debut after signing from Fulham for £650? The Fulham manager was sacked for allowing this signing.

96   Who became the first Reading player to be sent off in a league game at Elm Park, for throwing a punch against Millwall on Boxing Day 1934?

97   Which team beat Reading at Elm Park in January 1935 to end a record-breaking run of 55 home games without defeat?

98   What local product was it customary for Reading to present to visiting teams in the 1930s?

99   What colour shirts did Reading revert back to in 1938/39, for the first time since their inaugural season?

100   Who was appointed Reading manager in April 1939? His highly-talented son joined the club soon afterwards as a result.

Quiz 11 – Cup Upsets *(Answers on page 105)*

101   Which Southern League team knocked Reading out in the 1st Round of the 1937/38 FA Cup?

102   How many First Division teams did Reading beat on the way to winning the Simod Cup in 1988?

103   Which team, at the time 4th in the First Division, did Reading beat 3-2 away in the League Cup in 1997?

104   Since Reading joined the Football League in 1920, who were the only non-league team to have beaten them at Elm Park?

105   Which Premier League team did Reading beat 3-1 at home in the 5th Round of the 2015/16 FA Cup?

106   Who scored Reading's goal to knock First Division Wolves out of the League Cup at Elm Park in 1978?

107   Which Division Three team knocked Reading out of the FA Cup twice in two years in the first decade of the 21st century?

108   Who did Matt Mills score against to ensure an FA Cup giant killing in 2011?

109   Which Premier League team did Reading beat on penalties at a subdued MadStad on 11th September 2001?

110   Which Southern League Premier team did Reading lose to in 1977/78, a year after knocking them out of the FA Cup?

Quiz 12 – Reading & Blackburn *(Answers on page 105)*

111 Who scored a spectacular late winner for Blackburn in the first ever Premier League meeting of the two clubs?

112 In the 2016/17 season Reading did the double over Blackburn, scoring the same number of goals in each game. How many?

113 Which striker joined Royals from Blackburn in January 2012 and kick-started that season?

114 Who scored two early goals for Reading in the 2-2 draw at Ewood Park in August 2018?

115 Name the winger who scored his final Reading goal against Blackburn in May 2007.

116 Which Reading player received a red card against Blackburn in the March 2008 0-0 draw at the MadStad?

117 Which Reading player was substituted with a broken hand early in the final match of the 2006/07 Premier League season, at Ewood Park?

118 Who scored Reading's two late goals in their 4-2 defeat at Blackburn in October 2007?

119 Reading's biggest win of 1986/87 was over Blackburn. What was the score?

120 Which two midfielders joined Blackburn on from Reading in August 2015?

Quiz 13 – World War II Royals *(Answers on page 106)*

121 What pricing innovation were Reading the first Football League club to introduce at the start of the 1939/40 season?

122 Which wartime competition did Reading win in 1940/41?

123 And who did Reading beat at Stamford Bridge in the final of this competition?

124 Reading recorded home and away wins over Arsenal in 1940/41. Where did Arsenal play their home games when Reading beat them this season?

125 Which European Cup-winning manager guested 40 times for Reading in wartime matches, and nearly joined the club as assistant manager?

126 By what score did Reading beat Watford in their first home match of 1943/44?

127 Which footballing great - and later Reading manager - saw his career as a player ended as the result of a spinal injury suffered against Reading in March 1945?

128 How many goals did Tony McPhee score from his 42 War League and Cup games for Reading in 1940/41?

129 Who did Reading beat 6-5 in January 1940 after being 5-1 down early in the game?

130 Which Reading player, who signed in May 1939 but never actually played for the club, died as a result of injuries suffered during the D-Day landings?

Quiz 14 – Top Scorers *(Answers on page 106)*

131 Who is Reading's all-time Football League top scorer?

132 Who scored 16 hat-tricks or better in wartime matches for Reading?

133 Which Reading player was Division Three's top scorer, despite playing for a team that was relegated?

134 Against which team did Trevor Senior score a four-minute hat-trick on his home debut?

135 How many goals did Trevor Senior score in his first season at the football club?

136 Who scored goals in eight successive league matches for Reading in 1930/31?

137 The highest number of penalties scored by Reading in a single season is 11, shared between Shane Long and who else?

138 Which Reading player scored 35 league goals in 1993/94, making him the highest scorer across all four divisions?

139 Which team did Reading beat 10-2 in 1946 to give them their highest league victory?

140 Reading lost both of the two highest-ever scoring Premier League matches. How many goals in total were scored in them?

Quiz 15 – Reading & Bournemouth *(Answers on page 106)*

141   Which ex-Reading player made his Premier League debut for Bournemouth against Everton in September 2019?

142   Two strikers have been Reading's top scorer in their first full season after signing from Bournemouth. Name them both.

143   When Reading hosted Bournemouth in May 2001 in the last match of the season, what was the score?

144   And how would Reading's history have been different if Bournemouth had won that match?

145   Reading last won at Bournemouth in April 2001. Who scored Reading's two goals that day?

146   And which striking prodigy scored Bournemouth's goal?

147   Which full-back joined Bournemouth from Reading in June 2013?

148   Which Reading substitute was sent off in the 76th minute of the 3-1 defeat at Bournemouth in September 1999?

149   And which two Reading players scored own goals for Bournemouth in that match?

150   Which Reading goalkeeper joined Bournemouth on a free transfer in 2015?

Quiz 16 – Post-War Biscuitmen *(Answers on page 107)*

151   Which Reading legend made his league debut for the club in the first home match of 1946/47 - seven years after joining the club?

152   Who scored four goals as Reading beat Palace 10-2 in 1946?

153   What communications device, funded by the Supporters' Club, was first used at Elm Park in October 1946?

154   During the "big freeze" of 1947, how did Reading fans show their disapproval of an Ipswich defender's robust tackling?

155   Who was the club's top scorer for the first time in 1949/50, scoring 22 league goals?

156   At which ground did Reading's FA Cup visit in November 1948 set an attendance record of 19,072, one never beaten?

157   Which ex-England international was appointed Reading manager in May 1947?

158 Which future high-profile player and TV pundit was given an amateur contract at Reading in 1948 but not offered a professional one?

159 Who did Reading break their transfer record to sign for £4,000 from Cardiff City in 1949?

160 Which ex-international and Division One winner was the star attraction when a crowd of close to 30,000 packed Elm Park to watch him play for Notts County in September 1949?

Quiz 17 – Goalkeepers *(Answers on page 107)*

161 From which club did Reading sign Marcus Hahnemann?

162 Which on loan 'keeper made the first of his five disastrous Royals appearances away at Crewe in 1998 in a 1-0 defeat?

163 Which Royals goalie was fans' player of the season in 1995?

164 Who scored an own goal to end Steve Death's record-breaking period without conceding a goal?

165 Which Dutchman kept goal for Reading in their first match at the Madejski Stadium?

166 Which Reading 'keeper's performance at Anfield was described as "absolutely staggering" by Brendan Rodgers?

167 Who replaced Steve Death in goal for the last 14 games of the 1975/76 season?

168 What nationality is João Virgínia, signed on loan from Everton in 2019/20?

169 Against which club did Nick Hammond save three penalties in an FA Cup shoot-out at Elm Park in 1998?

170 Which goalkeeper holds the club record for most consecutive Reading appearances, 156?

Quiz 18 – Reading & Brentford *(Answers on page 107)*

171 Which striker did Reading sign from Brentford for a then-record fee of £800,000 in August 1997?

172 What competition did Reading win by beating Brentford 3-2 at Stamford Bridge in 1941?

173 In which minute of the final match of the 2001/02 season, away at Griffin Park, did Jamie Cureton score his crucial equaliser?

174 Which centre-back did Reading pay £350,000 to Brentford to sign in July 2006?

175 Which Reading player received a red card late in the 2-1 home defeat to Brentford between Christmas and New Year 2015?

176 Name the two Reading wingers who joined Brentford on free transfers in consecutive summers, 2003 and 2004.

177 Which two members of the 106 point squad joined from Brentford?

178 How many spectators watched Reading host Brentford at Elm Park in February 1927 to set the attendance record for that ground?

179 Who scored twice in Reading's 2-2 draw at Brentford in September 2018?

180 Who replaced Steve Coppell as Brentford manager when he left the club in June 2002?

Quiz 19 – Reading in the 1950s *(Answers on page 108)*

181 The FA Cup visit of which First Division team in 1954/55 was Elm Park's first-ever all-ticket match?

182 Which Reading striker was dropped for the first 10 games of 1950/51, but when recalled scored 35 goals in the remaining 36 matches?

183 Reading finished second in Division Three (South) in 1951/52. Which team finished above them in the table?

184 Which team did Ted Drake suddenly leave Reading to become manager of in May 1952?

185 Which future manager signed for Reading as a professional in September 1953?

186 Who were the opponents in Reading's first floodlit Football League match at Elm Park in February 1956?

187 Why was it unusually important that Reading finished in the top half of the table in 1957/58?

188 Who was Chesterfield's goalkeeper when they visited Elm Park in January 1959?

189 Which radio service broadcast matches live from Elm Park for the first time in 1957?

190 Who was Reading's top league scorer in 1957/58, with 24 goals from 42 games?

Quiz 20 – League Cup (1) *(Answers on page 108)*

191 Which goalie made his only Reading appearance as Reading lost at Leeds in the 1995/96 League Cup?

192 Reading received a bye in the 1992/93 League Cup as a result of which club's bankruptcy?

193 Who scored for Middlesbrough to controversially knock Reading out of the League Cup quarter-finals in January 1998?

194 And who was the referee who signalled the free-kick to Reading that was taken by Boro?

195 Who knocked Reading out of the 2019/20 League Cup, 4-2 on penalties?

196 Which team were Reading drawn against three times in consecutive years in the late 1990s?

197 Which Division One team did Reading beat 5-4 on aggregate in a two-legged League Cup 2nd Round tie in 1987/88?

198 And who scored both Reading goals in the away leg?

199 Who scored Newcastle's fourth goal as they beat Reading 4-0 at St. James's Park in October 1989?

200 Who did Reading lose 5-3 to in their first ever League Cup match?

Quiz 21 – Reading & Brighton *(Answers on page 108)*

201 How many league visits did Reading make to the Withdean Stadium?

202 Which midfielder joined Brighton from Reading in August 2016?

203 Who scored a hat-trick for Reading in their 5-1 home defeat of Brighton in December 2005?

204 Whose deflected free-kick gave Reading a 1-0 victory at Falmer in April 2012 – one of their only two shots on target?

205 Which Reading player was red-carded in his team's 2-1 away League Cup win over Brighton in September 2016?

206 In the 1974/75 League Cup, how many times did Reading and Brighton meet before the tie was resolved?

207 Who was the Brighton chairman who allowed Reading to speak to Steve Coppell in 2003?

208 Which Reading striker made 81 league appearance for Brighton between 2014 and 2018?

209 The scorer of Brighton's first goal in their 2-1 win at the MadStad in April 2003 would join Reading the following season. Name him.

210 Who scored the two goals that gave Reading a 2-0 win at the Withdean in the 2005/06 team's first away match?

Quiz 22 – Reading in the 1960s *(Answers on page 109)*

211 Two Chelsea and England players trained at Reading as youngsters in the early 60s - name them both.

212 In which competition did Reading play their first games in 1960/61?

213 In 1960/61 Reading won just one away league match all season. Where?

214 What match scheduling experiment did Reading trial in 1961/62 to try to increase falling attendances at Elm Park?

215 Which Reading player became the only goalkeeper ever to score two goals in a Football League match, in a 4-2 win over Halifax in 1962/63?

216 Which London Division One team did Reading beat 3-1 away in the League Cup in October 1964?

217 Which First Division team thrashed Reading 7-0 at Elm Park in an FA Cup 3rd Round replay after a goalless away tie?

218 Who scored four goals in a 7-0 home win over Hartlepool in August 1968?

219 How many substitutions were made by Reading in the 1965/66 season, the first they were permitted?

220 Which Reading player retired in 1966 due to persistent knee injury, but then stayed with the club for another 43 years?

Quiz 23 – Managers (1) *(Answers on page 109)*

221 Which Reading manager had previously captained Ted Drake's First Division Title winning team of 1954/55?

222 In the 21st century, five permanent managers have lasted less than a year in the role. Name them?

223 What derogatory name was Terry Bullivant known by, a reference to his former profession?

224 Which Reading manager is commemorated by a plaque at the Madejski Stadium and the name of a lounge at the Kassam Stadium?

225 Which Reading manager won a Champions League winner's medal as a player?

226 Name a Reading manager who has scored an FA Cup winning goal.

227 Who is Reading's longest-serving manager, with seven years in the job?

228 Who was caretaker manager for 13 days in December 2015?

229 Which manager resigned after Reading's relegation from Division Two in 1931?

230 Who recommended to Steve Coppell that he become Reading's next manager in 2003?

Quiz 24 – Reading & Bristol Clubs *(Answers on page 110)*

231 Who scored a 90th minute equaliser at Ashton Gate and was then sent off for his celebrations in Brian McDermott's first match as Reading manager, in December 2009?

232 Which two Bristol Rover players scored six second-half goals between them at the Madejski in January 1999?

233 In 1989/90 Reading needed two replays to get past Bristol Rovers in the FA Cup 1st Round. Who scored their single goal in both replays?

234 Who is the Welsh international who joined Reading on a free transfer from Rovers in July 1992?

235 The signing of which player from Bristol City was Reading's first £1M transfer?

236   In the two legs of the 1986/87 League Cup 1st Round, Reading scored six goals against Bristol Rovers. Trevor Senior scored five of them, but who got the other?

237   Who scored two goals in the last five minutes to give Reading a 3-2 away win over Bristol City in January 2017?

238   Which winger, signed from Bristol City in July 2003 re-signed for them just nine months later.

239   Whose cheeky 90th minute back-heel secured Reading a 3-2 win away at Bristol City in September 2011?

240   Which Bristol City manager came onto the Elm Park pitch in 1984 to appeal for calm amongst his club's rioting fans?

Quiz 25 – Reading in the 1970s *(Answers on page 110)*

241   In 1970/71, in what competition did Reading host Man Utd?

242   What event in the town prompted Reading to become "The Royals" in 1976?

243   Which Reading manager was sacked in October 1971 following a series of defeats and two players being suspended for a breach of club discipline?

244   After winning promotion to it in 1975/76, how many seasons did Reading successfully survive in Division Three?

245   Which Reading player missed part of the 1972/73 season after being injured playing for Canada in a World Cup qualifying match?

246   Who was the first black player to play for Reading, in October 1972?

247   Which "Minty" player did Reading sign from Bury in 1974?

248   What was unusual about Reading's first goal of the 1975/76 season, at home to Rochdale?

249   By what score did Reading beat Tranmere in the 1975/76 promotion run-in?

250   Who was manager of the Lincoln side that was Division Four champion in 1975/76?

Quiz 26 – Sendings Off *(Answers on page 110)*

251   Which Sheffield United player was sent off at The Madejski just 10 seconds after coming on?

252   Who came on as a Reading substitute in the 72nd minute of their match at Old Trafford and was shown a straight red card in the 73rd?

253   Two Reading "Andies" were sent off at Ipswich in March 1998. Name them both?

254   How many red cards did the record-breaking 2005/06 team receive?

255   Who was the West Ham player who lost his cool in December 2011 and was sent off after Jimmy Kebe pulled his socks up?

256   Who received Reading's first red card of the 2019/20 season, in a 4-1 home defeat to Fulham?

257   Which Reading player was sent off at Bradford in April 2004 after an altercation with Dean Windass?

258   Which on loan full-back was sent off as Reading hosted Manchester City at the Madejski in March 1999?

259   Which Reading player was sent off for two bookable offences in Reading's first ever league match at Old Trafford?

260   Which Reading player was sent off in the away play-off semi-final in 2017?

Quiz 27 – Reading & Burnley/Preston *(Answers on page 111)*

261   Which two wingers did Reading sign from Burnley in the first decade of this century?

262   Who scored Reading's last-minute winner over Preston at the Madejski in December 2019?

263   Who scored two goals in Reading's 3-0 win at Deepdale in August 2005?

264   How many goals did Burnley put past Reading in the clubs' first league meeting at Turf Moor in September 1930?

265   Preston inflicted Reading's record defeat in an FA Cup 1st Round tie in 1894. What was the score?

266   In February 2003, Reading beat Burnley 5-2 at Turf Moor. Which two Reading players scored two goals each?

267 Which Reading striker did Tommy Burns sign from Birmingham after he had agreed terms with Preston?

268 Which Reading player joined Burnley three months after being dramatically sent off against them?

269 How did Reading infuriate Preston's players, supporters and ground-staff before the match at Deepdale in February 2000 - at the instigation of Martin Allen?

270 Which Reading striker joined Burnley for £35,000 in July 1991?

Quiz 28 – 1978/79 Season *(Answers on page 111)*

271 Which former Reading centre-half played much of this season up front, scoring nine league goals in the process?

272 Who did Reading host in the League Cup 4th Round, in front of a crowd of 25,046?

273 And what was notable about an away supporter ejected by police amidst crowd trouble during the above match?

274 Reading's back four missed only two league games between them all season. Name these four players.

275 Which team from a higher league did Reading knock out of the FA Cup in the 1st Round?

276 Who scored all four goals in Reading's crucial 4-0 win over title-rivals Grimsby in March 1979?

277 Four Reading players scored ten or more league goals this season - name them.

278 Which Southampton midfielder joined the club on loan in March 1979, following an injury to Richie Bowman?

279 Who did Reading beat 5-1 at home in February 1979?

280 To whom did Reading lose 1-0 away on March 24th - the last goal conceded by the team that season?

Quiz 29 – Royals in Europe *(Answers on page 111)*

281 Who played just 87 minutes of action for Reading - and the following season was a UEFA Europa League winner?

282 Which team did he win the Europa League with?

283 Which two Reading players played alongside each other in the Bundesliga?

284 Where did Reading spend their pre-season tour in 2005/06?

285 Which ex-Royal was an unused substitute in the 1991 European Cup Winners' Cup Final?

286 Which national team did Reading beat 2-0 in May 1913?

287 Which future Reading signing spent a season on loan at Beşiktaş in Turkey early in his career in 1988/89?

288 Which team beat Reading Under-23s 3-1 to deny them a place in the Premier League International Cup Final in April 2019?

289 By what margin did Reading miss out on UEFA Cup qualification at the end of the 2006/07 Premier League season?

290 Which future-Royal scored for Real Madrid against Milan in the 2009/10 Champions League?

Quiz 30 – Reading & Cambridgeshire *(Answers on page 112)*

291 We all know it was a bargain price, but how much did Reading pay Cambridge for Dave Kitson in 2003?

292 What was the score when Peterborough hosted Reading in the League One Cup in August 2013?

293 Which Reading substitute was himself substituted after just 17 minutes on the pitch at the Abbey Stadium in April 2001?

294 Which long-standing player scored one of his four Reading goals in their 3-2 League Cup win over Peterborough in 2012, only his third Reading match?

295 Who was Reading's scorer in their last League victory over Cambridge, in September 2001?

296 Reading have met Peterborough more times than any other opposition in the League Cup. How many times?

297 Who scored his only goal of the season in Reading's crucial win over Cambridge which clinched promotion in 1975/76?

298 And who was the Cambridge manager that day?

299 Which striker joined Reading from Cambridge in February 2000 for £750,000?

300 Who scored a brace in Reading's 6-0 Championship win over Peterborough in April 2010?

Quiz 31 – 1979/80 Season *(Answers on page 112)*

301   Reading full-back Gary Peters departed the club in the summer of 1979. Which club did he join?

302   Which Reading coach was forced to play his first match for 30 months in Reading's first league match of 1979/80 due to an injury crisis?

303   Maurice Evans broke the club's transfer record three times this season. Who was the first of these three signings, arriving from Crewe for £25,000?

304   Which team did Reading thrash 7-0 at Elm Park between Xmas and New Year this season?

305   And what did their manager, Allan Clarke, do to his team as a punishment for that defeat?

306   Who was named as a substitute at the age of 16 - Reading's youngest ever - although he was unused at the time?

307   Which Reading midfielder finished the season with 11 league goals - just one behind top league scored Mike Kearney?

308   Which local-born centre-half made his Reading debut in February 1980, just a few days after his seventeenth birthday?

309   What did Reading players have to do after matches for the first time this season?

310   Who played in all 54 of Reading's matches this season, and received a testimonial match against "Young England" in November 1979?

Quiz 32 – FA Cup (1) *(Answers on page 112)*

311   Which Premier League team have Reading played 15 FA Cup games against, more than against any other opponent?

312   What year did Reading first enter the FA Cup?

313   Against which Division One club did Reading force two replays in the 1st Round of the FA Cup in January 1920/21?

314   Which non-League club knocked Reading out in the 2nd Round of the 1977/78 FA Cup?

315   Which ex-Royal's goal knocked Reading out of the 2019/20 FA Cup?

316   Which team's 5th Round visit in February 1927 set Elm Park's attendance record of 33,042?

317 Who scored Reading's only ever FA Cup semi-final goal?

318 Who scored Manchester City's goal to defeat Reading in the 2010/11 6th Round?

319 Who scored goals in the 3rd, 4th and 5th Rounds in 2009/10 as Reading knocked out three Premier League sides?

320 Whose volley against the crossbar in stoppage time of an FA Cup replay at home to Manchester United nearly brought a dramatic equaliser in 2007?

Quiz 33 – **Reading & Cardiff City** *(Answers on page 113)*

321 Who was sent off for Reading in their last ever league meeting at Ninian Park?

322 How many goals did Reading put past Cardiff in each of their two league matches in 2005/06?

323 And which Cardiff player scored against Reading in both of those 2005/06 matches?

324 Which ex-Royal captained Cardiff in the Premier League?

325 Who scored two of Reading's three goals in their 2011 play-off final win at Cardiff?

326 And who scored the third - an outstanding solo effort?

327 In what year was a female steward assaulted at Elm Park by Cardiff fans during trouble at a 4th Round FA Cup replay?

328 Reading beat Cardiff 3-2 at Ninian Park in March 2004. Who scored their late winner?

329 Who scored twice for Reading in their 3-0 home win over Cardiff in August 2019?

330 Which unlikely player scored Reading's last minute equaliser against Cardiff at the MadStad in December 2008?

Quiz 34 – **1980/81 Season** *(Answers on page 113)*

331 Which Reading player joined Chester for a short while but then rejoined Reading a few months later. He was to stay with the club in various roles until 2013.

332 Which player joined from Spurs in July 1980?

333 Which winger was converted to full-back by Maurice Evans to cover for injuries – and only moved back to the wing in the last three years of his Reading career?

334 Which 19-year-old was Reading's top scorer with 13 goals in his first season as a professional?

335 How many goals did Reading score in their four matches in December 1980?

336 Admission prices for the South Bank rose by over 20% this season, amid much complaining from supporters. To what figure?

337 Which Second Division team knocked Reading out of the League Cup?

338 Which centre-back returned to the team in August 1980 after a year's break due to injury?

339 Who replaced Steve Death between the posts for Reading for the last six matches of this season?

340 Who became Reading's youngest ever goalscorer this season?

Quiz 35 – Reading at Wembley *(Answers on page 113)*

341 How many times have Reading played at Wembley?

342 In how many of these matches did Reading score first?

343 Which ex-Reading player made his debut for his new Premier League club in a match at Wembley?

344 Which member of Reading's backroom staff was "sent off" at half-time at Wembley?

345 Who scored Reading's first ever Wembley goal?

346 What is Reading's aggregate extra time score from matches played at Wembley?

347 In what competition did Michael Gilkes represent Reading at Wembley in 1992?

348 And where did he finish?

349 Which ex-Royal scored the winning FA Cup final goal at Wembley in the same year as Reading's Simod Cup triumph?

350 How many goals have Reading scored in total at Wembley?

Quiz 36 – **Reading & Chelsea** *(Answers on page 114)*

351 Chelsea visited Elm Park for a pre-season benefit match for who in August 1988?

352 Whose late own goal gave Reading a 2-2 draw at Stamford Bridge on Boxing Day 2006?

353 Who did Chelsea purchase from Reading in September 2015 but never actually select to play a match?

354 Reading beat Chelsea 7-2 in a Wartime League Cup match in March 1943. Who scored a hat-trick for them?

355 Which player was sent off on his Reading debut, at home to Chelsea in 2007?

356 Which two new signings both scored their first Reading goals away at Chelsea in August 2012?

357 How many Premier League matches did Steve Sidwell start for Chelsea?

358 Which Chelsea defender started his second loan spell with Reading in July 2019?

359 Who came off the bench to score two late goals to level the Premier League match against Chelsea in January 2013?

360 How many goalkeepers did Chelsea use in their first Premier League visit to Reading?

Quiz 37 – **1981/82 Season** *(Answers on page 114)*

361 Which youngster was Reading's top scorer this season, with 15 league goals?

362 Why was Reading's points total in twelfth place higher than Rotherham's total in winning the league the previous season?

363 In which early-season competition introduced this season did Steve Hetkze score a hat-trick against local rivals Aldershot in August 1981?

364 To whom did Reading lose 6-1 in February 1982?

365 Which long-serving player walked away from the club in February 1982 following a property dispute with them?

366 Why did Neil Webb miss five games from September 1981?

367 Which Reading striker scored eight goals in 18 league matches but then left the club and the UK to join his American wife?

368 Which goalkeeper, recruited from Andover due to an injury crisis, played his only game for Reading in the 1-1 draw against Swindon in February 1982?

369 And what was unusual about both the goals in that match against Swindon?

370 Against which team did Reading score four goals at home and concede four away from home in league matches this season?

Quiz 38 – Robin Friday *(Answers on page 114)*

371 From which club did Reading sign Robin Friday?

372 Against which team did he make his Reading Debut?

373 Against which club did Friday score a phenomenal goal in a 5-0 win at Elm Park in March 1976?

374 And who was the World Cup referee who said it was the best goal he'd seen in his whole career?

375 After scoring a last minute tap-in against Rochdale at Elm Park in April 1974, how did Friday celebrate?

376 Why was Friday arrested by British Transport Police upon arrival at Cardiff to sign for his new club?

377 Which Cardiff-based band released a single about Friday in 1996, entitled "The Man Don't Give a F*ck"?

378 How many league goals did Friday score in his 121 league appearances for Reading?

379 What did Reading fans vote Friday as in 1999?

380 While playing for Cardiff, which Brighton defender did Friday receive a red card for kicking in the face?

Quiz 39 – Reading & Crystal Palace *(Answers on page 115)*

381 Reading's highest league victory came over Palace in 1946. What was the score?

382 Which influential midfielder joined Reading from Palace in August 1994 for £90,000?

383 Who scored a hat-trick to help Reading win 4-2 against Palace in August 2008 at the Madejski?

384 How many spells as Palace manager did Steve Coppell have?

385 Who scored the decisive winning goal in Reading's dramatic 3-2 win over Palace at the MadStad in September 2005?

386 Palace signed two Reading players when they were promoted to the Premier League in 2013. Name them both.

387 Who scored twice for Reading in their 2-2 draw at Selhurst Park in March 2004?

388 Which Reading centre-back was sent off as his team lost 2-0 at home to Palace in the 2015/16 FA Cup?

389 Which international midfielder joined Reading from Palace on a free transfer in 1997?

390 How did Reading fans taunt Palace's goalkeeper Julian Speroni in the 0-0 draw at Selhurst Park in March 2009?

Quiz 40 – 1982/83 Season *(Answers on page 115)*

391 In the summer of 1982 Neil Webb left the club for a record fee of £87,500. Which club did he join?

392 In the first League Group Cup match of the season, what new rule did Lawrie Sanchez fall foul of when he was sent off after 21 minutes?

393 How many goals did Kerry Dixon score in the 7-5 defeat at Doncaster in September 1982?

394 What was the attendance for Reading's 3-2 home defeat to Preston at Elm Park in October 1982 - the lowest for a league match at Elm Park?

395 Ian Gillan was linked as a potential purchaser of Reading. For which rock band had he been lead singer?

396 What did Chairman Frank Waller announce minutes after Reading's home draw against Gillingham in April 1983?

397 Which club did Reading meet five times this season - twice in the league, once in the League Group Cup and twice in the two-legged League Cup 1st Round?

398 How many goals did Kerry Dixon score in all competitions this season?

399 Which player scored twice in his first two games for Reading whilst still a serving in the army?

400 Who did Reading play at home in the last match of the season, needing a win plus favourable other results to avoid relegation?

Quiz 41 – "Thames Valley Royals" *(Answers on page 116)*

401   What did Reading fans walk behind along Oxford Road on the way to the match against Millwall in April 1983?

402   Who was the tycoon and publisher behind the whole "Thames Valley Royals" scheme?

403   Which ex-Reading player, by this time a property developer, came forward to purchase the football club?

404   Near which town was the suggested new stadium for "Thames Valley Royals" going to be located?

405   Which Reading director placed a High Court injunction which stopped the immediate sale of Frank Waller's shares?

406   Sixteen days after the scheme was announced, Reading played their penultimate away match of the season, away at Oxford Utd. What was the score in that match?

407   Which national newspaper did Maxwell own?

408   Which third Football League team did Maxwell have a controlling interest in, registered in his son, Kevin's name?

409   In which month in 1983 was the merger finally rejected by the Reading FC board, although it was clear it had failed several months before this meeting?

410   How is Roy Tranter commemorated for his successful efforts to halt the merger?

Quiz 42 – Reading & Derby County *(Answers on page 116)*

411   Which Reading striker did Derby pay a fee of over £3M for in January 2016?

412   A win by how many goals against Derby at Pride Park on the last day of the 2007/08 season would have saved Reading from relegation?

413   When Reading beat Derby 2-1 at Pride Park in the 2015/16 FA Cup 5th Round, which Derby player was sent off?

414   Which Pole joined Reading from Derby in 2012 but made just four appearances?

415   In April 1986 Reading hosted Derby at Elm Park in what was billed as a "title decider." What was the final score?

416   Which player scored his first Royals goal from the penalty spot in his team's 3-0 win over Derby in December 2019?

417 Which promising young winger's only Reading appearance was against Derby in the last match of the 2014/15 season, a 3-0 away win which wrecked Derby's play-off hopes?

418 And which on-loan striker, who only played six times for Reading, scored an early goal in that match?

419 Which Reading player scored against Derby both home and away in the 2017/18 season?

420 Reading beat Derby 5-0 to confirm the Championship title in April 2006. Which Reading substitute scored two late goals?

Quiz 43 – 1983/84 Season *(Answers on page 116)*

421 What was the score in Reading's first home match of the season?

422 How many minutes were there between Trevor Senior's first and third goals in that match?

423 What substantial change to the team's home strip was made this season?

424 Who did Maurice Evans appoint as his assistant manager in pre-season of 1983/84?

425 Reading lost just one of their last 20 league games after the appointment of Ian Branfoot. To whom?

426 In how many League matches this season did Trevor Senior score two or more goals?

427 From which club did Dean Horrix sign for £10,000 in August 1983?

428 Whose stunning free kick in the last home match, against Tranmere, ensured Reading's promotion back to Division Three?

429 Which two teams finished ahead of Reading in the table this season?

430 Where was the final match of the season, where Trevor Senior scored twice to break Ron Blackman's record for most goals in a league season?

Quiz 44 – Sponsors *(Answers on page 117)*

431 Which local newspaper was the first Reading FC shirt sponsor, in 1982/83?

432 Which company provided Reading's shirts between 1977 and 1981?

433 Who sponsored the 0898 "Royalsline" premium rate recorded information service?

434 Who are Westcoast, the club's shirt sponsor for six years from 1999?

435 Which major shirt supplier did Reading switch to in 2004, and stay with for 15 years?

436 Who were the shirt sponsors of the 106 point promotion-winning team?

437 Which sponsor's name had to be covered up with tape - and why?

438 Who were the last UK-based company to sponsor Reading's shirts?

439 Many consider Reading's red and white away shirt of 1991/92 to be the best - or the worst - kit ever. It was certainly distinctive. But which company's name was on it?

440 Who sponsored Reading's Simod Cup Final shirts?

Quiz 45 – Reading & Everton *(Answers on page 117)*

441 Who scored Reading's single goal at Goodison Park in their FA Cup 5th Round win in March 2011?

442 Whose goals for Everton gave them a 2-1 3rd Round League Cup win in September 2015 at the Madejski?

443 From which club did Gylfi Sigurðsson join Everton?

444 Who scored Reading's consolation goal in the 3-1 Premier League defeat to Everton in March 2013?

445 Reading's home win over Everton in 2012/13 was their first Premier League win that season. How many matches had they played before this?

446 And who scored the two goals to give Reading this first win?

447 Which Reading goalkeeper signed a short-term contract with Everton but never played a game for them, before leaving to end his career overseas?

448 Who scored Reading's goal in the 1-0 Premier League win at home to Everton in August 2007?

449 How many games did on-loan Everton keeper João Virginia make for Reading in 2019/20?

450 Which Everton player scored against Reading both home and away in the two 2006/07 Premier League matches? He did the same for another club the previous season.

Quiz 46 – 1984/85 Season *(Answers on page 117)*

451 Which legendary Reading winger made his league debut this season?

452 What features were added at the back of the main stand this season?

453 Which two non-league teams did Reading face in the 1st and 2nd Rounds of the FA Cup this season?

454 Which other striker outscored Trevor Senior in early league matches, ending the season with 19 league goals compared with Senior's 22?

455 Which European Footballer of the Year was a guest player for Reading in a friendly at Elm Park in October 1984?

456 In February 1985, which full-back rejoined Reading for his second spell with the club?

457 Which team, winners of the Division Three title this season, did Reading beat 5-2 away in early May 1985?

458 Which on-loan striker scored twice in Reading's FA Cup win over Bognor?

459 In how many consecutive matches did Trevor Senior score one or more goals, equalling the club record?

460 What unique goalscoring record did Kerry Dixon complete this season?

Quiz 47 – Royals in Management *(Answers on page 118)*

461 Which ex-Reading centre-back spent four years in charge of Carlisle United?

462 Which club did Phil Parkinson start his managerial career with?

463 Which future global superstar was managed by Gary Peters for a brief spell of five matches in 1994/95?

464 Which ex-Royal lifted Northern Ireland's FIFA ranking from 124th to 33rd during his spell as manager?

465 Who was Charlton manager when Phil Parkinson joined them as assistant manager?

466 Where did Maurice Evans start his managerial career, in 1972?

467 Which Reading goalscoring hero managed Bradford City to promotion in his first season with the club, 1968/69?

468 Which ex-Royal spent seven years in charge of Western League Premier Division club Bridport from 2009?

469 Which Reading player managed Bury whilst aged only 30?

470 Which club in crisis did Kerry Dixon manage for a year from August 1996? It later transpired he wasn't allowed to pick the team, and only advised the chairman on team selection?

Quiz 48 – Reading & Fulham *(Answers on page 118)*

471 When Seol Ki-Hyeon moved to Fulham in August 2007, which player came to Reading as part of the deal?

472 Reading lost 5-0 to Fulham at Craven Cottage in December 2016. Which Reading player was red-carded early in the second-half in this match?

473 In May 2013 Reading gained their last Premier League victory at Craven Cottage. What was the score?

474 And who scored two goals for Reading in that win?

475 Which ex-Reading manager was also manager of Fulham between 1994 and 1996?

476 Who scored Reading's penalty to win the Championship play-off semi-final second leg against Fulham in May 2017?

477 And which Fulham player's handball meant that penalty was awarded to Reading?

478 Reading drew 1-1 with Fulham in the first home league game of the 2017/18 season. Which Fulham player was sent off after just 39 seconds of the game?

479 Name the midfielder who joined Reading from Fulham for £100,000 in August 1999.

480 Which ex-Reading player gained promotion to Division Two with Fulham in 1981/82?

Quiz 49 – 1985/86 Season *(Answers on page 119)*

481 What started to be issued to Reading fans during the 1985/86 season?

482 Which full-back did Reading sign from Swindon Town for £22,500 in the summer of 1985?

483 Whose Football League record for consecutive wins at the start of the season did Reading beat in 1985?

484 And at which ground did Reading break this record?

485 Which midfielder scored the opening goal for Reading in this record-breaking game?

486 Who scored two goals for Reading in December 1985 as they came back from 3-0 down at home to Plymouth to win 4-3?

487 In February 1986 Reading paid a reported £87,500 for midfield enforcer Terry Hurlock. From which club did he sign?

488 Which player, signed this season, was rescued from unconsciousness by Reading physio Glenn Hunter after falling heavily in a league match at Swansea in February 1986?

489 Which club did Reading beat 1-0 in their penultimate home match to virtually guarantee winning the Division Three title?

490 Which member of Reading's 1925/26 title-winning team was on the pitch as the 1985/86 title was awarded to Reading?

Quiz 50 – Transfer Trails (2) *(Answers on page 119)*

Name the Reading player from their transfer history. The number of league appearances made for Reading is shown in brackets.

491 Dunstable > Reading (116) > Chelsea > Southampton > Luton Town > Millwall > Watford > Doncaster Rovers

492 Arsenal > Brighton (loan) > Aston Villa > Everton > Arsenal > Leicester City > Reading (5)

493 Reading (218) > Nottingham Forest > Ipswich Town

494 Portsmouth > Aldershot (loan) > Reading (164) > Watford > Middlesbrough > Reading (137) > Woking

495 Oxford City > Slough Town > Bromley > Nottingham Forest > Reading (234)

496 Reading (196) > Wolves > Reading (loan) (15) > Reading (122) > Coventry City > Millwall (loan) > Swindon Town

497 Crystal Palace > Brentford > Reading (155) > Hull City > Wolves > Ipswich Town > Coventry City

498 Cork City > Reading (174) > West Bromwich Albion > Hull City > Southampton

499 Oldham Athletic > Notts County > Reading (168) > Norwich City > Leeds United > Scunthorpe United > Charlton Athletic > Bolton Wanderers

500 Grenoble > Brentford > Reading (127) > Stoke City > Hull City (loan) > Portsmouth (loan) > Ipswich Town > Akhisar Belediyespor > Harlow Town

Quiz 51 – Reading & Humberside *(Answers on page 119)*

501 Which Reading captain signed from Hull City in July 2015?

502 In March 1979, which Reading striker scored all four goals in the 4-0 home win over Grimsby Town?

503 Which left back joined Reading from Scunthorpe in May 2010 but only made three appearances for the club?

504 Who scored for Reading against Hull both home and away in the 2005/06 Championship winning season?

505 Which player scored his first Reading goal at home to Grimsby in April 2003, in the first of three spells with the club?

506 Which Reading manager started his management career at Scunthorpe and was most recently manager at Hull?

507 In September 2018 Reading beat Hull 3-0 at the Madejski but had a player sent off in the 84th minute. Who?

508 Mick Gooding & Jimmy Quinn's first signing, a record at £250,000, left to join Grimsby in July 1997. Name him.

509 Which Reading midfielder's late goal, one of only two he scored for the club, ensured a 1-0 League Cup win for Reading at Scunthorpe in August 2014?

510 Which member of the 106 point squad departed Reading for Hull City in August 2009?

Quiz 52 – 1986/87 Season *(Answers on page 120)*

511 Which player did Ian Branfoot sign from Chelsea for £60,000 in the 1986/87 pre-season?

512 In August 1986 Reading visited Bristol Rovers in the League Cup, playing the first match played at the ground Rovers had recently moved to. Name it.

513 Which Oldham striker punched Martin Hicks in an off-the-ball assault, breaking his jaw, in a League match at Elm Park in October 1986?

514 In Reading's next home match, that Oldham striker's twin brother Paul received continual abuse from Reading supporters and was eventually sent off for lashing out at Trevor Senior. Which club did he play for?

515 Which player did Reading sign on trial to replace Hicks? He was sent off 27 minutes into his Reading debut and only played five matches before being released.

516 Who was the Reading goalkeeper whose crisis of confidence led to him being replaced by Steve Francis?

517 Reading lost 3-1 at home to Arsenal in the 3rd Round of the FA Cup. Who was Reading's outstanding player in the game, running rings around England full-back Kenny Sansom?

518 When Steve Francis was concussed in the Easter Saturday match at home to Portsmouth, which Reading player took over in goal?

519 In the last home match of the 1986/87 season, Reading triumphed 2-0 over the Division Two champions-elect to ensure their own survival. Which team did they beat?

520 Which Reading player was sent off in the 23rd minute of this final home match of 1986/87?

Quiz 53 – Famous Fans *(Answers on page 120)*

521 Which journalist, wine connoisseur and cricket commentator was a Reading FC supporter?

522 Which Goodie now follows Reading, in tribute to a fans' song about him?

523 Who was the self-proclaimed psychic who failed to demonstrate his powers at Elm Park in February 1995 when Reading fans didn't hold up coloured cards as he had predicted?

524 Which former 5-Live travel reporter was never reticent about proclaiming her support for Reading FC while on air?

525 Which fictional middle-manager said: "Guilty! I support Reading"?

526 Who is the Reading-supporting actress famous for roles in *Game of Thrones* and *The Hunger Games: Mockingjay Parts 1 & 2?*

527 Which critic and television presenter, arts critic for *The Guardian* and later *The Sunday Times*, and twice named "Critic of the Year," is a Reading supporter?

528 Reading supporter Irwin Sparkes is the lead singer with which pop rock band?

529 Which Oscar winner grew up in a house a stone's throw from Elm Park?

530 Which Reading fan might ask if this is your final answer in this round?

Quiz 54 – Reading & Ipswich Town *(Answers on page 120)*

531 Which on loan Norwich striker scored his last goal for Reading in their 2-1 win over Ipswich at Portman Road in March 2019?

532 Which Reading full-back went in goal during the league match at Portman Road 19 August 1996 after Reading's 'keeper was sent off late in the first half?

533 And who was the Reading goalkeeper sent off in that match?

534 How many Royals in total were sent off in the club's four league games at Portman Road between 1996/97 and 2003/04?

535 Which Reading striker joined Ipswich on a free transfer in June 2005?

536 And which Reading centre-back did the same six years later?

537 How many of the "Magnificent Seven" signed by Tommy Burns on transfer deadline day 1998 started in the match at Portman Road just two days later?

538 All four matches between the clubs in 2003/04 and 2004/05 ended up with the same score. What was it?

539 What was significant about Reading's 3-0 win at Ipswich on 22nd November 2005?

540 In September 2015, which player scored a hat-trick as Reading beat Ipswich 5-1 at home?

Quiz 55 – 1987/88 Season *(Answers on page 121)*

541   Home-grown centre-back Steve Wood left Reading in the 1987/88 pre-season. Which club did he join?

542   Against which Spanish club on the team's pre-season tour did Ian Branfoot draft in five fans to make up the numbers due to injuries to players?

543   Which former player did Reading face in their two League Cup 2nd Round matches?

544   Which centre-back joined Reading from Bristol City for £150,000 in October 1987?

545   Which team knocked Reading out of the FA Cup in the 3rd Round with a narrow 1-0 win at Elm Park in January 1988?

546   Which new signing this season scored seven league goals in six matches in October 1987, but ended the season with only eight goals from his 20 league matches?

547   Which team did Reading meet in both the League Cup and the Simod Cup this season?

548   In February 1988 Billy Whitehurst was purchased to try to provide goals to keep Reading up. Where did he join from?

549   How many league matches out of their 44 did Reading win this season?

550   Who did Reading meet in their last match of the season at Elm Park? They needed to win to have any chance of staying up but could only draw 0-0.

Quiz 56 – The Simod Cup *(Answers on page 121)*

551   Who are Simod?

552   Who did Reading beat in their first Simod Cup match of 1987/88?

553   And which full-back, playing in midfield, scored two goals for Reading in that win?

554   Who scored the winning goal in extra time to beat Brian Clough's Nottingham Forest side at Elm Park in the 3rd Round?

555   Which Reading striker, transfer-listed at the time, scored for Reading in the 2nd, 3rd and 4th Rounds of the Simod Cup?

556 Who scored the final, winning penalty for Reading in the semi-final shoot-out at Elm Park?

557 And which goalkeeper did he beat with that penalty?

558 Which two long-serving Reading players were brought on as substitutes in the final at Wembley?

559 Which player scored the first goal in the Simod Cup final?

560 Which member of the winning Reading team had previously won this trophy, then known as the "Full Members' Cup"?

Quiz 57 – **Reading & Leeds** *(Answers on page 122)*

561 In December 2011, Reading beat Leeds 1-0 at Elland Road, through a goal scored in the 2nd minute. By whom?

562 Who spent 13 months as manager of Leeds, in between two spells in that role with Reading?

563 Who scored the winning goal in Reading's 3-2 League Cup victory over Leeds in November 1997?

564 From which club did Reading sign ex-Leeds player Ian Harte?

565 Which Reading midfielder had his ankle broken in a match against Leeds at the Madejski in April 2012?

566 And who was the Leeds manager that day?

567 Which promising young goalkeeper did Leeds pay Reading £300,000 to sign in March 2000?

568 Which ex-Reading winger spent five months on loan at Leeds in 2014, scoring once in his nine league appearances?

569 Who joined from Leeds in July 1993 and won a Division Two winner's medal in his first season with Reading?

570 Who scored his second - and last - Reading goal in their 4-2 away win at Elland Road in March 2014?

Quiz 58 – **1988/89 Season** *(Answers on page 122)*

571 Which centre-back left Reading for a new club record fee in October 1988?

572 And which club paid this record fee for him?

573 Which Reading player was unexpectedly sold to Sunderland in September 1988, just four games into the season - said to be as the result of an incident in a Reading nightclub?

574 Trevor Senior rejoined Reading in October 1988. From which club?

575 What injury did Reading 'keeper Steve Francis suffer at home to Bristol Rovers in October?

576 And who replaced Francis in goal for 24 league games until he returned to the team in March 1989?

577 Why was the capacity of Elm Park reduced to 12,174 towards the end of the 1988/89 season?

578 Stuart Beavon was second highest scorer this season, with ten goals in all competitions. How many of these were penalties?

579 Which team did Reading need to beat to avoid relegation in the last match of the season?

580 In this last match of the season, Reading were 2-0 down at half-time. What was the final score?

Quiz 59 – Elm Park (1) *(Answers on page 122)*

581 Who scored the first goal at Elm Park, in a friendly against "Royston Bourke's London XI" in September 1896?

582 Why was the new main stand not completed in time for the start of the 1926/27 season?

583 Who were the visitors for Elm Park's lowest ever league attendance, 1,934, in April 1991?

584 Which world heavyweight champion boxer was part of an exhibition bout staged at Elm Park in June 1944?

585 What was the name of the supporters' social club at Elm Park?

586 Which international team used Elm Park as their training base during the 1948 Olympic Games?

587 In what year was a covering roof first provided along the whole length of the South Bank?

588 Which Channel Four drama series was filmed at Elm Park in the late 1980s?

589 Which French team were the visitors for Elm Park's first match under floodlights?

590 In what year was the Tilehurst Road end first concreted?

Quiz 60 – Reading & Leicester City *(Answers on page 123)*

591   Which striker did Ian Branfoot purchase from Leicester for a club record fee of £250,000 in November 1987?

592   Reading lost 2-1 at home to Leicester in the FA Cup 4th Round in January 2005. Which Reading player was shown a red card after 76 minutes in this match?

593   A Leicester winger joined Reading on loan in February 2004, and later joined on a permanent basis. Who was he?

594   Which member of the 106 point team, who made 11 league appearances that season, joined from Leicester in July 2005?

595   Mark McGhee failed to stop Leicester being relegated to Division Two in 1994/95. What was the score in their two league matches against Reading the following season?

596   In August 2016 a future Reading captain joined from Leicester. Name him.

597   Reading drew 1-1 with Leicester at the Madejski on Easter Monday 2014. Who scored their goal that day?

598   And who was the Reading midfielder was sent off in that Easter Monday match?

599   Which former Reading trainee followed Mack McGhee to Leicester in July 1995?

600   What date was Reading's most important league meeting with Leicester?

Quiz 61 – 1989/90 Season *(Answers on page 123)*

601   Which non-league team did Reading need three replays to overcome in the 2nd Round of the FA Cup?

602   In their first league match of this season, Reading drew 3-3 at home. With whom?

603   Which team knocked Reading out of both the FA and League Cups, scoring four goals at home in both ties?

604   Which match was Ian Branfoot's last in charge of Reading?

605   Who spent 22 days in charge as Reading's caretaker manager?

606   Who was appointed Reading's new manager in November 1989? He had spent five matches on loan at Reading in 1976.

607   Which club did Reading host at home in the FA Cup in their first match in the 1990s?

608 How many FA Cup matches in total did Reading play this season?

609 Which former Reading favourite was tragically killed in a car accident in March 1990, at the age of only 28?

610 Which Reading full-back scored three goals this season - all in the FA Cup?

Quiz 62 – Chairmen and Owners *(Answers on page 123)*

611 Which long-serving chairman resigned in acrimonious circumstances in May 1954?

612 Which chairman proclaimed "We want promotion - and quickly" upon taking up the role in 1968?

613 And what was the name of the Woodley-based engineering company of which he was president?

614 Which Reading chairman made 59 appearances for the club in two spells in the 1960s and 70s?

615 Who supposedly purchased Reading FC, but is reported to have never put any money into the club and left the board after just over two years?

616 What is the name of the operating company of Reading owner Dai Yongge?

617 In what year did John Madejski purchase Reading FC?

618 And how much did he pay for his 51% controlling interest?

619 Who was the co-chairman responsible for the much-ridiculed club song "They Call Us the Royals"?

620 Why did Frank Waller quit as chairman in May 1983?

Quiz 63 – Reading & Liverpool *(Answers on page 124)*

621 In what competition did Reading's first ever meeting with Liverpool happen, and when?

622 What was the score in this first match between the clubs?

623 In 2007/08, Liverpool met Reading in the League Cup and again scored four goals, winning 4-2 at the Madejski in September. Who scored a hat-trick for them?

624 Which Liverpool centre-back joined Reading for a reported £3.75 million in January 2017?

625 Who scored both of Liverpool's goals as they beat Reading 2-0 in the clubs' first league meeting at Anfield?

626 Whose goalkeeping heroics earned Reading a clean sheet at home to Liverpool in April 2013 - as well as rave reviews for his performance?

627 Which Reading player scored a first-half own goal to give Liverpool the lead in the FA Cup 3rd Round replay at Anfield in January 2010?

628 Who crossed the ball for Shane Long to score his extra time winner in the FA Cup 3rd Round replay at Anfield in January 2010?

629 And which Liverpool player did he spectacularly nutmeg before crossing?

630 Who scored his only Premier League goal for Reading with a spectacular strike from 20 yards at Anfield in March 2008?

Quiz 64 – 1990/91 Season *(Answers on page 124)*

631 Why did a number of Reading stewards spend time in Italy in the summer of 1990?

632 Which striker did Reading purchase from Huddersfield Town in August 1990?

633 And why was the size of the transfer fee this player a nasty shock to Reading?

634 In September 1990, Trevor Senior's goal in the match away at Rotherham broke whose Reading FC goalscoring record?

635 And in October 1990, Martin Hicks's 537th appearance saw him break which player's record for most Reading appearances?

636 Which Reading cult hero died in December 1990?

637 Who scored on his first league start for Reading, a 1-0 home win over Fulham on 1st December 1990?

638 And what was significant about this match against Fulham?

639 For what two reasons was Ian Porterfield sacked as manager in April 1991 - apart from the team's on-field performance?

640 Who recommended to John Madejski that he should appoint Mark McGhee as manager, in May 1991?

Quiz 65 – Play-offs (2) *(Answers on page 125)*

641   Which of Reading's six home play-off semi-finals had the biggest attendance?

642   Who fouled Nathan Dyer to earn Swansea their first penalty of the 2011 final?

643   Who was the first player to fail to score in the 2017 play-off final penalty shoot-out?

644   Which Reading player suffered the indignity of giving away a penalty, getting a straight red card - and failing to get his shirt off over his head?

645   Which Reading winger was sent off in the 2003 play-off semi-final, first leg?

646   For how many minutes was Nicky Forster on the pitch against Wigan in the home play-off semi-final of 2001?

647   Which record-breaking goalkeeper was on the bench for Bolton in 1995?

648   Which Reading substitute was sent off at half-time in the play-off final vs. Swansea?

649   Which Reading player was fouled by Bolton's Jason McAteer to give Reading a penalty at Wembley in 1995?

650   Which is the only one of Reading's play-off finals not to go to extra time?

Quiz 66 – Reading & Local Rivals *(Answers on page 125)*

651   Which Reading player was sent off when Reading last met Swindon Town in the league, a 0-0 draw at The County Ground on Valentine's Day 2002?

652   Reading beat Aldershot 4-0 at Elm Park in April 1979. Which ginger-haired striker scored two of Reading's goals?

653   In their two 2001/02 league meetings, Reading beat Wycombe 2-0 home and away. Which Reading striker scored in both of these matches?

654   Reading beat Oxford 4-3 at home in October 2000. Whose two late goals sealed the win?

655   Which Reading Simod Cup winner was Wycombe's manager when Reading beat them 3-2 away in October 1998?

656 Reading beat Swindon 2-0 at Elm Park in October 1996. Who scored both of their goals?

657 Reading lost to Wycombe 5-3 at Adams Park in October 1999. Name the Reading goalkeeper substituted at half-time.

658 Reading knocked Oxford out of the League Cup in August 2004 with a 2-0 away win. Who were their scorers?

659 Which Swindon centre-back joined Reading in January 2011?

660 By what score did Reading knock Aldershot out of the FA Cup 1st Round in December 1967?

Quiz 67 – 1991/92 Season *(Answers on page 125)*

661 Which club record signing left on a free transfer to Exeter in August 1991?

662 Which local non-league club did Reading need two attempts to defeat in the 1st Round of the FA Cup in November 1991?

663 Which midfielder joined the club on trial in August 1991? Except for a one-year spell at Stevenage, he would stay with Reading in various roles until May 2009.

664 Which Chelsea defender scored five goals from his five matches on loan to Reading in January 1992?

665 Which player regained his position as Scotland's number one goalkeeper after rescuing his career with 11 outstanding appearances on loan at Reading?

666 And which Scottish international striker made a single on-loan appearance for Reading, against Huddersfield at Elm Park in January 1992?

667 Which scoring milestone did Trevor Senior reach when he scored the winner in that game against Huddersfield?

668 After not scoring in five league games, who did Reading beat 6-1 at Elm Park in April 1992?

669 Which Reading player took part in a Wembley final this season?

670 Who spent part of his last game for Reading in goal as an emergency 'keeper, after Steve Francis went off injured?

Quiz 68 – Premier League Royals *(Answers on page 126)*

671 For how many teams has Steve Sidwell made Premier League appearances?

672 Which ex-Reading youngster played nine Premier League matches for Nottingham Forest in the competition's first year?

673 Which ex-Reading loanee has hardly missed a Premier League match for Bournemouth since joining them in June 2017?

674 Which former Reading player's Premier League debut came in a 3-2 win over Arsenal, with him providing the assist for the winning goal?

675 For which team has Kevin Doyle scored the most Premier League goals?

676 For which team did Keith Curle make 131 Premier league appearances between 1992 and 1996?

677 Which ex-Reading youngster has scored 28 Premier League goals from 124 appearances for West Ham up to March 2020?

678 Which player made 221 Premier League appearances for three different clubs over an 11-year period after leaving Reading?

679 Which winger made 31 Premier League appearances for a London club before joining Reading, and nine Premier League appearances for a different London club after leaving them?

680 Which Reading trainee, later to rejoin the club, scored a single Premier League goal in two seasons with West Brom from 2010?

Quiz 69 – Reading & Luton Town *(Answers on page 126)*

681 Which Reading player sustained an injury away at Luton in March 1999 that was to keep him out of the team until the following October.

682 Reading beat Luton 5-1 at home in the League Cup in August 2008. What was notable about their first two scorers?

683 Who was Luton's goalkeeper in the Simod Cup final - beaten four times by Reading?

684 One of Reading's worst ever signings joined from Luton for £500,000 in March 1999. Name him.

685 What did Luton do in February 2006 that no other club did against Reading that season?

686 Which Reading player was booked for simulation in this match?

687 And which ex-Reading player scored the third goal for Luton?

688 Who scored a Reading hat-trick as they beat Luton 4-1 in December 2000?

689 Which promising youngster did Jaap Stam allow to join Luton on a free transfer in June 2017?

690 Luton were the first visitors to the MadStad in August 1998. What was the score in that match?

Quiz 70 – 1992/93 Season *(Answers on page 126)*

691 Which First Division team did Reading host in a pre-season friendly, in front of 10, 497 fans - their biggest home attendance since the week of the Simod Cup Final?

692 Why did Reading progress to the 2nd Round of the League Cup without having to play a match?

693 Mark McGhee made four significant signings in July 1992, one of them a free transfer from Bristol Rovers. Name him.

694 And from which club did Phil Parkinson sign for £37,500 in July 1992?

695 Which 17-year-old made his debut for Reading in the 1-0 FA Cup victory over Birmingham?

696 Which French club took him on trial as a result of his performance in this game?

697 Reading drew 1-1 with Manchester City in the FA Cup 3rd Round in January 1993. Who scored Reading's goal?

698 Which two teams did Reading beat 4-0 in the league at Elm Park in this season?

699 One of the new summer signings ended the season as top scorer with 23 goals. Who was he?

700 Why could you say that McGhee's decision to sign a player in September 1992 was not rocket science?

Quiz 71 – Sir John Madejski *(Answers on page 127)*

701   What was John Madejski's birth name?

702   And where was he born, in 1941?

703   Name the original title of the publication with which he founded his publishing empire.

704   What did John Madejski call his publishing company?

705   Where in London is the "John Madejski Garden" located?

706   In what year was he knighted?

707   What does John Madejski famously collect?

708   With which singing star was he romantically linked by the press in 2004?

709   To what company did Madejski sell his 51% interest in Reading FC in 2012?

710   At what institution would you find the "John Madejski Fine Rooms"?

Quiz 72 – Reading & Manchester City *(Answers on page 127)*

711   In January 1993, by what score did Manchester City beat Reading in their FA Cup 3rd Round replay at Elm Park?

712   Reading's home defeat on Manchester City at Elm Park in February 1998 was their penultimate win of the season. What was the margin of victory?

713   Alan Pardew's last permanent signing for Reading arrived from Manchester City in August 2003. Name him.

714   In December 2012's Premier League meeting at the Etihad Stadium, a dogged Reading defensive performance was ruined by a 90th- minute Manchester City goal. Who scored it?

715   In February 2007, Reading won their first Premier League match at the Etihad Stadium through two almost identical goals. Who scored them both?

716   Which Reading starlet was said to have turned down a £2M move to Manchester City in April 2014?

717   In which round of the FA Cup did Reading lose to Manchester City 1-0 in March 2011?

718   Manchester City were the opposition for Reading's second home Premier League match, in September 2007. What was the score in that game?

719 Reading beat Manchester City 2-0 in their home league match in October 1996. Who scored both of Reading's goals?

720 Which player, signed for City for £10M by Mark Hughes in January 2009, ended his playing career at Reading?

Quiz 73 – 1993/94 Season *(Answers on page 127)*

721 Which long-serving full-back left the club in the summer of 1993, after making 380 league appearances?

722 And which full-back was signed from Leeds in July 1993 as a replacement for him?

723 Goalie Steve Francis was allowed to leave the club in the summer of 1993 as he'd lost his first-team place. Which club did he join for £15,000?

724 What was the score in Reading's league match away at Exeter in October 1993?

725 And which three Reading players all scored two goals each?

726 Who was Reading's "German Sub", who saw action after coming off the bench in nine league matches this season?

727 In how many league matches this season did Reading score four or more goals?

728 Jimmy Quinn was top English scorer this season. How many did he score?

729 Against whom did Reading earn the points that ensured promotion?

730 Which Reading player earned his first international cap in May 1994?

Quiz 74 – Transfer Trails (3) *(Answers on page 128)*

Name the Reading player from their transfer history. The number of league appearances made for Reading is shown in brackets.

731 Enfield > Leytonstone/Ilford > Brentford > Reading (29) > Millwall > Rangers > Southampton > Millwall > Fulham

732 Reading (227) > Hibernian > Livingston > Queen of the South

733 Reading (212) > Northampton (loan) > Bournemouth (loan) > Norwich City (loan) > Southampton (loan) > Derby County > Bristol City (loan) > Millwall (loan) > Millwall

734 Livingston > Sheffield United > Portsmouth (loan) > Bradford City (loan) > Coventry City > Reading (15) > Hibernian (loan) > Sunderland (loan) > Hibernian (loan)

735 York City > Reading (306) > Charlton Athletic (loan) > Southampton

736 Crystal Palace > Swansea City (loan) > Coventry City > Bolton Wanderers (loan) > Fulham > Charlton Athletic > Reading (111) > Brentford

737 Wimbledon > West Ham United > Cardiff City > Crystal Palace > Watford > Reading (189) > Leyton Orient > Stevenage > Leyton Orient

738 Bishop Auckland > Rotherham > Chesterfield > Rotherham > Peterborough > Wolves > Reading (314) > Southend

739 Tottenham Hotspur > Notts County (loan) > Reading (396) > Northampton > Newbury Town

740 Arsenal > Brentford (loan) > Beveren (loan) > Brighton (loan) > Reading (168) > Chelsea > Aston Villa > Fulham > Stoke City > Brighton (loan) > Brighton

Quiz 75 – Reading & Man Utd. *(Answers on page 128)*

741 Which Reading player was sent off in the team's first ever League match at Old Trafford?

742 Reading have played Man Utd. 15 times in the FA Cup but have won only once. When?

743 In August 2007 United's Wayne Rooney suffered a third broken metatarsal after an accidental stamp from which Reading centre-back?

744 Which Reading player, signed from Manchester United in June 1998, scored his first two goals for the Royals at the Madejski Stadium in August 1998?

745 Who scored two late goals to cement United's 4-0 FA Cup 3rd Round win over Reading in January 2017?

746 Who were the goalscorers in Reading's first Premier League clash with Manchester United, in September 2006, a 1-1 draw?

747 Which on-loan Man Utd. player appeared for Reading in both home and away play-off semi-finals in May 2003?

748 Which player, later to join Reading, was sent off in Manchester United's 5-3 Premier League defeat to Leicester in September 2014?

749 What was the score after six minutes in Reading's 3-2 defeat to Manchester United in the FA Cup 5th Round replay in February 2007?

750 Which member of United's "Class of 92" made just two first-team appearances for United before joining Reading in 1998?

Quiz 76 – 1994/95 Season *(Answers on page 129)*

751 From which club did Dariusz Wdowczyk join Reading in August 1994?

752 Which Olympic gold-medallist trained with Reading in the summer of 1994, and scored a goal in a friendly against Leatherhead?

753 Why was Reading's home game against Notts County in October 1994 halted for 17 minutes during the second half?

754 Who did Reading meet at Elm Park in the first match after Mark McGhee's departure, in a match televised by ITV?

755 Which striker joined from Watford in January 1995 and scored ten league goals from 20 appearances?

756 In February 1995 Reading beat Middlesbrough 1-0 in their last visit to Ayresome Park. Who scored Reading's goal?

757 Against which team did Stuart Lovell score a hat-trick on April Fool's Day 1995?

758 Who did Reading beat 2-1 at home in their penultimate league match of the season? Played on a Friday, capacity was reached before kick off with many fans unable to get in.

759 Who did Reading host in their last league match of the season, and what was the score?

760 Who was Reading's leading scorer in this season?

Quiz 77 – Assistant Managers *(Answers on page 129)*

761 Which player-Manager of the reserves scored 143 league goals in his playing career at Reading?

762 Lew Chatterley was assistant to which Reading manager, and spent 22 days in temporary charge following his dismissal?

763 Who was assistant manager to Mark McGhee, and followed him to Leicester City?

764 Which former Reading assistant manager took over from Wally Downes as Brentford manager in 2004?

765 Which assistant manager took charge of the club for four matches in 1991? He was given a police warning over his behaviour in a match at Griffin Park during this spell.

766 At which ground did Martin Allen cause a rumpus by instructing the players to warm up in the same half as the home team?

767 Who was assistant manager to Brian McDermott at both Reading and Leeds?

768 Which former Spurs full-back was assistant manager to Brendan Rodgers at Reading?

769 Which Reading assistant manager had formerly been Jock Stein's last signing for Celtic in 1978?

770 Which assistant manager of the England team later became Reading's assistant manager?

Quiz 78 – Reading & Middlesbrough *(Answers on page 129)*

771 Which two Reading players scored twice in their 5-2 Championship win over Middlesbrough in March 2011?

772 And who scored Boro's two goals in that game?

773 Which Middlesbrough player clattered Dave Kitson in the club's first ever Premier League match in August 2006, putting him out for nearly five months?

774 Which notable international star played an hour for Boro in their last league visit to Elm Park on Easter Monday 1998?

775 And which Boro player was sent off in this match for a horrible foul on Reading's Paddy Kelly?

776 How much did Middlesbrough pay Reading to sign Leroy Lita in August 2009?

777 Reading drew 1-1 at home to Boro in the Premier League in December 2007. Who scored Reading's goal?

778 Which on loan striker scored his only goal for Reading in a 2-1 defeat at the Riverside Stadium in February 2018?

779 Who was the only player to make his Reading debut in their match at home to Boro in August 2006?

780 And how many Reading players made their Premier League debuts in this match?

Quiz 79 – 1995/96 Season *(Answers on page 130)*

781 In pre-season, Simon Osborn was one of three players to leave for record sums. To which club did he depart, for a fee of £1.1M?

782 And which player moved in the opposite direction 12 days later, as a potential replacement for Osborn?

783 In September 1995 Reading purchased Boris Mihaylov. Which goalkeeper, signed from Watford the previous year, was he signed to replace?

784 After struggles to make the pitch playable, Reading hosted Manchester United in the FA cup 4th Round in January 1996, losing 3-0. Who scored United's second goal, a mishit cross that went in at the far post?

785 Why could Reading consider themselves lucky to beat Bury 2-1 in the 3rd Round of the League Cup at Elm Park in November 1995?

786 And who scored the winning goal against Southampton in the League Cup 4th Round in November 1995 with an 88th minute header - despite having had four steel plates inserted into his skull a few months earlier?

787 Which team did Eric Nixon make his only Reading appearance against in the League Cup 5th Round tie in January 1996?

788 Which two players were signed by Reading in February 1996? One broke Reading's transfer record and the other was to play a significant role in Reading's history.

789 Mark McGhee made his first return to Elm Park when he brought his Wolves team for the last home game of the season in April 1996. What was the score in this game?

790 How many players played in goal for Reading in the 1995/96 season?

Quiz 80 – World Cup Royals *(Answers on page 130)*

791 For which country had Boris Mihaylov made a reported 82 international appearances when Reading signed him?

792 Which Reading player started two of his team's matches in the group stages of the 2006 World Cup?

793 And which teammate of his was an unused substitute in those three group games?

794 In which match at Italia 90 did Neil Webb make his only World Cup finals appearance?

795 Who was the only Reading's player at that time to participate in the 2018 World Cup finals in Russia?

796 Which future Reading player scored a memorable late equaliser against Italy in the knockout stages of the 2002 World Cup?

797 Which Reading player holds his national team's record for most caps, but has never featured at the World Cup finals?

798 Which goalkeeper, who played five matches during a loan spell at Reading, was an unused substitute at both the 1986 and 1990 World Cup finals?

799 Which ex-Royal scored in his country's first ever World Cup finals appearance?

800 Which player made his final international appearance in a 1998 World Cup play-off decider in November 1997, four months after joining Reading?

Quiz 81 – Reading & Millwall *(Answers on page 131)*

801 Which member of the Reading 2012 promotion-winning squad left to join Millwall in January 2015?

802 In their League Cup meeting in August 2017, Reading beat Millwall 3-1 after extra time. Who scored their two extra time goals?

803 Which writer and broadcaster played for both Millwall and Reading? In 2002 he "ghost-wrote" the autobiography of Roy Keane.

804 In August 2005 which Reading player scored a memorable goal, running the full length of the pitch before scoring, in a 5-0 home win over Millwall?

805 In Reading's first home league game of 2011/12, Reading drew 2-2 with Millwall thanks to two goals in the last four minutes. Who scored them?

806 And which former Reading player scored Millwall's first goal in this season opener?

807 Which player, signed from Millwall in October 1978, scored eight goals from 16 league appearances to help Reading win the 1978/79 Division Four title?

808 In January 2020 Millwall beat Reading 2-0 at the New Den. Which ex-Royal scored their second goal?

809 In the 0-0 draw with Millwall at The Den in April 1985, how many Reading players were booked by Referee Martin Bodenham?

810 Which former Royal scored Millwall's second goal to help his team beat Everton in the FA Cup 4th Round in January 2019?

Quiz 82 – 1996/97 Season *(Answers on page 131)*

811 Ady Williams left Reading in a £750,000 move in July 1996. Which club did he join, and which central defender was signed from Wrexham nine days later to replace him in the team?

812 Against which team was Andy Bernal sent off in the first match of the season?

813 Andy Bernal also received a red card against Barnsley in the Reading's third league match of the season. Which Reading player was also sent off in their second match, away at Ipswich?

814 To whom did Reading lose 6-1 at Elm Park in the league in September 1996?

815 Reading beat Southampton 3-1 in the FA Cup 3rd Round at Elm Park in January 1997. Who was the Southampton manager who had to be physically prevented from confronting the referee at the end of the match?

816   Which team did Reading beat 3-2 at Elm Park in February 1997, an especially satisfying win for all home supporters?

817   Who scored all three of Reading's goal in that match?

818   In which minute of the 2-1 home defeat of Mark McGhee's Wolves team did Stuart Lovell score Reading's winning goal, thus ensuring Reading were safe from relegation?

819   And injuries to which Wolves player led to so much time being added on in that match?

820   Which Reading player suffered a serious knee injury in the team's defeat to Aylesbury in the Berks and Bucks Senior Cup Final in May 1997?

Quiz 83 – Managers (2) *(Answers on page 131)*

821   At which ground is there a bronze memorial celebrating the career of Tommy Burns?

822   Two Reading managers had brief spells as caretaker manager at least a year before being given the role permanently. Name them.

823   Which ex-Reading manager has been frequently criticised by Matt Le Tissier for dropping him because "I didn't run about like a headless chicken enough?"

824   Which former England international became Reading manager in January 1963?

825   Against which team did Alan Pardew score the winning goal for Crystal Palace in the 1989/90 FA Cup semi-final?

826   With which club had Steve Clarke been discussing their managerial vacancy before he was dismissed by Reading?

827   Who joined Reading as manager in 1939 but had his contract terminated after just four matches?

828   Which Reading manager went on to manage clubs from two different countries in the Champions League?

829   Who replaced Ted Drake as Reading manager in 1952?

830   At which club was Nigel Adkins promoted to manager from his role of club physiotherapist?

Quiz 84 – Reading & Newcastle *(Answers on page 132)*

831 Who scored twice for Reading in their first Premier League meeting with Newcastle, in December 2006?

832 Prior to that match, Reading had not met Newcastle in a competitive match since their FA Cup 4th Round replay meeting in January 1990, when Newcastle triumphed 4-1. Who scored Reading's single goal in that game?

833 Who scored two goals for Newcastle in this 4-1 home FA Cup victory, and also the 3-3 draw at Elm Park which led to this replay?

834 Which former Magpie pulled out of Reading's squad to play Sunderland on the grounds that "his head was not in the right place" at the time?

835 Which striker, who joined Reading from Newcastle as one of the "Magnificent Seven" in March 1998, scored one goal from his 42 league appearances for Reading?

836 Another member of the "Magnificent Seven" also joined from Newcastle. Who was he?

837 Who scored Reading's goal as they beat Newcastle 1-0 at the Madejski in the Premier League in April 2007?

838 Which ex-England striker played for Newcastle in that Premier League match, but failed to impress?

839 In their second Premier League meeting at the Madejski, in October 2007, Reading again beat Newcastle, 2-1, with Newcastle's goal being scored by a Reading player. Name him.

840 Reading beat Newcastle 2-1 at St James's Park in the Premier League in January 2013. Which Reading striker came off the bench to score twice in six minutes?

Quiz 85 – 1997/98 Season *(Answers on page 132)*

841 Who turned down an offer to manage Reading in the summer of 1997, preferring to join the coaching staff at Newcastle?

842 From which club did Terry Bullivant join Reading as manager in June 1997?

843 And which two players did he sign from his old club in August 1997?

844 Against which team did Reading achieve their first league win in September 1997, their seventh league match of the season?

845 Reading beat Mark McGhee's Wolves 4-2 in the 4th Round of the League Cup at Elm Park - inevitably! Who scored Reading's second goal, a cracker from 25 yards?

846 Which goalkeeper, on loan to Reading, played in five league games, all defeats, in which he conceded 16 goals and Reading scored one?

847 What was Terry Bullivant's last match in charge of Reading?

848 How many of the 13 players who played in Tommy Burns's first match in charge, away at Ipswich in March 1998, were making their Reading debuts?

849 How many points did Reading win from their last 17 league matches of the season?

850 How many players in total did Reading use in all competitions this season?

Quiz 86 – Ups and Downs *(Answers on page 133)*

851 Since joining the Football League in 1920 how many promotions and relegations have Reading had?

852 How many times have they been promoted as champions?

853 What is Reading's lowest ever points total from a season of league football?

854 Since 1920 how many times have Reading finished second in the league and not been promoted?

855 What was Reading's lead over the third-place team when they were promoted with 106 points in 2005/06?

856 Since 1920, how many times have Reading finished bottom of the league table?

857 In which year were Reading relegated on goal average?

858 In the 62 seasons since Division Four was introduced in 1958/59, at which level of the pyramid have Reading spent the most seasons?

859 In which season did Reading gain 53 points from a 46-game season but still get relegated?

860 What is Reading's lowest ever end-of-season position in the Football League pyramid?

Quiz 87 – Reading & Non-League Teams *(Answers on page 133)*

861   From which non-league team did Maurice Evans sign Kerry Dixon?

862   Who was the Wealdstone substitute whose bad tackle on Martin Hicks in a 1985/86 FA Cup tie, only moments after coming onto the pitch, sparked a 20-man brawl?

863   From which team, in National League North in 2019/20, did Reading purchase Tony Barras for £20,000 in March 1999?

864   Which team did Reading beat 6-3 at Elm Park in March 1970? They were voted out of the Football League two season later to be replaced by Hereford United.

865   Which local non-league team's proposed groundshare with Reading was scrapped in 1990 after the Vauxhall Premier League decreed that Elm Park did not meet their required standards?

866   Which now-defunct team did Barry Hunter join from Reading in September 2001, later becoming their manager?

867   At which ground did a surge of Reading fans celebrating a 120th minute extra time goal to win a League Cup 1st Round tie cause a wall to collapse in August 2011?

868   And who scored that goal in the last minute of extra time?

869   With which team, now defunct and re-formed, did Reading draw 3-3 in the League Cup in September 2006?

870   From which now-defunct team did Reading sign Steve Swales in July 1995?

Quiz 88 – 1998/99 Season *(Answers on page 133)*

871   The last match played at Elm Park, in August 1998, was a pre-season testimonial for which long-serving club employee?

872   Which player joined Reading from Manchester United in June 1998 for a fee of £300,000?

873   Which Liberian player made the assist for Brebner to score the first goal at the Madejski Stadium in August 1998?

874   Tommy Burns sentenced five players to train with the reserves in the middle of the 1998/99 season. What were they popularly known as?

875   Reading signed a Dutch goalkeeper on 1st August who played just four matches for them - the last of them on 22nd August in the first match at the Madejski. Name him.

876   Which player claimed the first hat-trick at the Madejski Stadium in January 1999?

877   Reading beat Manchester City 1-0 at Maine Road in October 1998, with Martin Williams scoring their goal. Which Manchester City player was sent off after 20 minutes?

878   Which team's visit to the Madejski in March 1999 saw the first crowd in excess of 20,000 to watch a Reading home match since 1978?

879   Which winger, signed from Dundee United two days previously for £100,000, was one of four new signings to make their debut in this match?

880   Which player, signed in the summer of 1998, made just nine league appearances this season due to a number of injuries?

Quiz 89 – Referees *(Answers on page 134)*

881   Which referee sent off Francis Benali and Robbie Slater - and then manager Graeme Souness - in Southampton's FA Cup defeat at Elm Park in January 1997?

882   Referee Keith Stroud stopped play in an away league match against Millwall in January 2020. For what reason?

883   Which referee apologised to Chris Gunter after wrongly booking him for diving in a league match at Blackburn in November 2013?

884   Which official, at the time the youngest ever Premier League referee, awarded Reading a "ghost goal" in a match at Watford in September 2008?

885   Who was the referee who deemed no foul had been committed despite Tyrone Mings's boot leaving Nelson Oliveria with multiple injuries when Reading hosted Aston Villa in February 2019?

886   In what year did Middlesbrough qualify for the semi-finals of the League Cup at Reading's expense due to poor refereeing from George Cain?

887 Who did Mike Riley send off in Reading's Premier League match at home to Newcastle in April 2007 on the grounds that he was confusing the linesman?

888 Who was the referee who awarded Sheffield United's Keith Gillespie the Premier League's fastest ever red card and also sent off Neil Warnock and Wally Downes in a fiery match at the MadStad in January 2007?

889 And who was the referee whose report led to Sheffield United manager Neil Warnock being charged with bringing the game into disrepute as a result of incidents in his team's match at the Madejski one season earlier?

890 Which referee was censured for failing to penalise Jermain Defoe for encroaching as Spurs took a penalty against Reading in December 2007?

Quiz 90 – Reading & Norwich City *(Answers on page 134)*

891 In April 2017 Reading were trounced 7-1 at Carlow Road. Who scored Reading's only goal?

892 Which former Norwich Player of the Season played for Reading in the last league match at Elm Park?

893 And which Norwich player scored the only goal in that final match?

894 Which Royals defender scored twice as his team won 2-1 away at Norwich in November 2014?

895 Which player signed for Reading from Norwich in August 1999, making 29 league appearances and scoring once?

896 In March 1954 Reading and Norwich played a high-scoring draw in a Division Three (South) match at Elm Park. What was that score?

897 Which Reading striker scored three times in the two league games against Norwich in 2008/09 - twice in the away game and once at home?

898 A former Norwich 'keeper spent five matches on loan at Reading in 1995. Who was his permanent club at the time?

899 Which fans' favourite at Reading was signed by Norwich manager Peter Grant in July 2005?

900   Who scored his first goal for Reading after 90 minutes to rescue a point for Reading in their 2-2 draw with Norwich at Carrow Road in April 2019?

Quiz 91 – 1999/2000 Season *(Answers on page 135)*

901   Which young Reading midfielder tested positive for drugs in July 1999?

902   Which Bristol City player, making his debut for the club in the first match of the season at the MadStad, deliberately kicked the ball into the home crowd, breaking a supporter's wrist?

903   What was Tommy Burn's last match in charge of Reading?

904   "Pants Day" was held at the MadStad on 18th December 1999. What did "PANTS" popularly stand for?

905   On Boxing Day 1999, a bad tackle by which Cardiff player in Reading's 1-0 defeat at Ninian Park effectively ended Chris Casper's playing career?

906   Where was Reading's first match of the new century?

907   And which on loan player scored Reading's first goal of the 21st century, after 87 minutes of this match?

908   The arrival of attacking full-back Matt Robinson in January 2000 revitalised Reading going forward. From which club did Reading sign him?

909   Who returned to Reading in the first of two loan spells in February 2000, after more than three and a half years away?

910   Which Reading midfielder was the team's highest scorer, with 23 goals this season?

Quiz 92 – Alan Pardew *(Answers on page 135)*

911   Which match was Alan Pardew's first in charge of Reading FC?

912   Which team beat West Ham in the Championship play-offs in Pardew's first season as their manager?

913   Who was Pardew's first signing as Reading manager?

914   West Ham saw Pardew as the replacement for which manager, who they sacked in August 2003?

915   Which manager brought Pardew from Yeovil to Crystal Palace in a £7,500 transfer in March 1987?

916   Who first took Pardew to Reading, as his reserve-team manager?

917   Who took over as caretaker manager of Reading following Pardew's departure?

918   And who was their first match against, three days after Pardew tendered his resignation but had it rejected?

919   With which team did Pardew end his league playing career?

920   What was the score in Pardew's last match as Reading manager, away to Wimbledon in September 2003?

Quiz 93 – Reading & Nottingham *(Answers on page 136)*

921   Which ace Reading goalscorer controversially joined Forest for a fee of £6,600 in 1954?

922   In the October 1997 3-3 draw with Forest at Elm Park, which Reading player scored a "wonder goal", beating four defenders before shooting home?

923   And which Forest player missed an embarrassingly open goal from short range in the first half of this match?

924   In the summer of 2001, Reading lost a midfielder to Notts County on a Bosman transfer - and acquired another from them a few days later. Name them both.

925   Reading beat Forest 4-3 in a thrilling match at The City Ground in April 2011. Who scored their last minute winner?

926   In their last visit to Meadow Lane in October 2001, Reading won 4-3, with all their goals coming in the first-half. Who scored two of them?

927   In 1901/02 Southern League Reading met Notts County for the first time, in an away FA Cup 1st Round match, and triumphed 2-1. What league were their opponents in that day?

928   County did not move to Meadow Lane until 1910. Where in Nottingham was this FA Cup 1st Round match played?

929   In July 2014 a former trainee rejoined Reading from Nottingham Forest. Name him.

930   In October 2016 Reading beat Forest 2-0 in a league match at the Madejski, with both their goals coming from players purchased from Forest. Who were they?

Quiz 94 – 2000/01 Season *(Answers on page 136)*

931 Which Reading striker suffered serious ligament injuries during Reading's last warm up match of the season, a friendly against Charlton in August 2000?

932 And who did Alan Pardew purchase to replace him, at a cost of £250,000?

933 Which Reading hero tragically died the day before the start of the season, in August 2000?

934 What did Reading fans chant to Oldham fans who had travelled over 200 miles to watch their team lose 5-0 at The Madejski, in September 2000?

935 How many goals did Reading score in their six league matches in September 2001?

936 Against which team did Reading recover from 3-2 down with 17 minutes left to win 4-3 at the Madejski in October 2000 - and which player scored their crucial two late goals?

937 With which club did Mark McGhee make his first visit to Reading's new stadium in January 2001?

938 Which Reading player scored his first goal for the club in the 3-1 defeat to Bristol City in March 2001?

939 Reading drew their last two home league games and, crucially, lost their last away match, condemning them to the play-offs. Where was this final away match of the season?

940 How many goals did Reading score in all competitions in this season?

Quiz 95 – Scottish Royals *(Answers on page 137)*

941 Which former Royal captained Livingston as they won the Scottish League Cup in 2004?

942 How many of Tommy Burns's "Magnificent Seven" were Scottish?

943 And which one of them went on to manage Dunfermline, Queen of the South, Ross County and Dundee between 2007 and 2019?

944 Which Scottish player left Reading in January 2000 after admitting problems with drug and alcohol addiction?

945 Which Reading player had a nine-match loan spell at Hibs immediately before joining Reading, and then signed for them permanently after just one season in Berkshire?

946 From which club did Scottish international 'keeper Jim Leighton spend 11 matches on loan in 1991/92?

947 With which Scottish team did Mark McGhee win the 1983 European Cup Winners' Cup and UEFA Super Cup, and three Scottish league titles?

948 Which player, signed by Tommy Burns in July 1998, went on to win four caps for Scotland?

949 Which Scot was sent off in Reading's FA Cup 4th Round match against Cardiff City in January 2020?

950 Which Scottish ex-Royal appeared in the film "The Damned United", playing his father?

Quiz 96 – Reading & Portsmouth *(Answers on page 137)*

951 Who scored two penalties for Portsmouth against Reading at Fratton Park in a 2-2 draw on Easter Saturday 1983?

952 Which team did Portsmouth lose to in May 2008, one week before they were due to play in the FA Cup Final, which meant that Reading were relegated from the Premier League?

953 Which defender left Reading to join Portsmouth in July 2000 and played 198 matches for them, becoming a Pompey hero in the process?

954 Reading's match against Portsmouth at Fratton Park in September 2007 set a new Premier League record. What record?

955 And who scored a hat-trick for Portsmouth in this match?

956 Which ex-Reading goalkeeper made 93 appearances for Portsmouth between 2002 and 2005?

957 And which ex-Reading 'keeper replaced him in goal for Portsmouth in 2004? He would make 109 Portsmouth appearances in all.

958 Which Reading player was sent off after just three minutes of his team's match with Portsmouth on New Year's Day 2008?

959 Within the space of eight weeks in early 1999, Alan Pardew purchased two players from Portsmouth. Name them both?

960 Which Reading hero unexpectedly joined Portsmouth in June 2008?

Quiz 97 – 2001/02 Season *(Answers on page 137)*

961 To which team did Reading lose 2-0 at the Madejski in a pre-season friendly which attracted a crowd of over 21,000?

962 Who made their first appearance on the Reading teamsheet in this season, wearing the number 13 shirt?

963 Pardew's ex-teammate John Salako signed for him in January 2002. From which club?

964 Who scored what was reported at the time the club's 5,000th Football League goal, in a 2-0 home win over Wycombe in September 2001?

965 Reading won seven consecutive league matches after Christmas 2001, scoring 14 times. How many goals did they concede in this winning run?

966 Which team dumped Reading out of the FA Cup in December 2001, for the second season running?

967 Reading were forced to play three matches in a week in February 2002, thanks to the demands of ITV Digital. Where were they on Valentine's Day in the third of these matches?

968 How many of their final ten league matches in March and April did Reading win?

969 In which minute of Reading's last match of the season, away at Brentford, did Jamie Cureton score the crucial goal that ensured promotion?

970 How many of the Brentford starting XI at Griffin Park that day would later sign for Reading?

Quiz 98 – Own Goals *(Answers on page 138)*

971 For which team did both Martin Hicks and Trevor Senior score own goals in their visit to Elm Park in November 1985?

972 Against which team did Nicky Shorey score his only Reading own goal, in a 3-1 away victory in April 2007?

973 Whose own goal against Aston Villa in May 1971 ensured that Reading were relegated?

974 Which Derby player scored an own goal, with a stunning volley, at Elm Park in February 1995 to give Reading a 1-0 win?

975 Whose head did Barry Hunter's clearance bounce off for an agonising own goal at Cardiff in May 2001?

976 Whose own goal gave Wolves a 75th minute equaliser in their home play-off leg against Reading in May 2003?

977 Reading drew 1-1 with Nottingham Forest at the Madejski in January 2020. Which Forest player scored a 97th-minute own goal?

978 Which Reading defender scored Portsmouth's sixth goal in their 7-4 home win in September 2007?

979 Reading beat table-topping Wolves at the Madejski 1-0 in January 2009 through a bizarre own goal. Who scored it?

980 Which Wolves player scored an own goal to give Reading the lead over Wolves in the 4th Round of the League Cup at Elm Park in October 1997?

Quiz 99 – Reading & QPR *(Answers on page 138)*

981 Which goalkeeper left Reading to join QPR in August 2014?

982 Who scored Reading's only goal in their 1-0 win over QPR at the Madejski on Boxing Day 2019?

983 Who was sent off playing for QPR as Reading beat them 1-0 at the Madejski in December 2004?

984 And what was called out to him that infuriated him so much?

985 Who scored Reading's second goal in their 2-1 home win over QPR in the 2005/06 Championship?

986 And what did Reading fans do before that match with QPR?

987 Which midfielder joined Reading from QPR in the summer of 2011?

988 In September 2012 Reading triumphed 3-2 over QPR in the 2nd Round of the League Cup at Loftus Road. Who scored their third goal in the 82nd minute?

989 In the 2017/18 season, Reading had players sent off against QPR in both home and away league matches. Name both players.

990 In what year did QPR first adopt blue and white hooped shirts?

Quiz 100 – 2002/03 Season *(Answers on page 138)*

991 Which international joined Reading permanently in August 2002, having spent six matches on loan at the club the previous season?

992 What funding crisis did Reading and other Football League clubs suffer in the summer of 2002?

993 Which defender joined Reading on loan in September 2002, and from which club?

994 In December, a Reading defender was accused of making a racist remark to an ex-Reading player. Name them both.

995 Who scored twice for Reading in his second match for them? Although under 20, he'd already played against Reading for two different teams.

996 In January 2003, against which team did Reading draw 0-0 away and then 1-1 at home in the FA Cup 3rd Round, before finally being knocked out on penalties?

997 Royals legend Phil Parkinson left Reading in February 2003. To join which club?

998 Against which team did Nicky Forster score a hat-trick at home in April 2003?

999 Which player made his only Reading appearance in the last away match of the season, at Watford, at the age of 16 years and 49 days to become Reading's youngest ever player?

1000 Whose injury in the play-off semi-final first leg at Molineux was a turning point in the game, with Reading leading 1-0 at that point?

Quiz 101 – Reading & Sheffield United *(Answers on page 139)*

1001 Which member of the 106 point team left Reading to join Sheffield United in January 2010 after a loan period on loan there?

1002 Who was the Sheffield United goalkeeper roundly abused by the Madejski crowd after not being sent off for handling the ball outside the box in the league match at the Madejski in October 2005?

1003 And which Reading player scored both the goals as his team won this match 2-1?

1004 Who joined Reading from Sheffield Utd in August 2008 and retired in 2011 due to multiple sclerosis?

1005 Which former Reading loanee scored for Sheffield Utd in their 2-0 league win at the Madejski in December 2018?

1006 In January 2007, in a home Premier League match, which full-back scored an outstanding goal for Reading against Sheffield Utd after a mazy run from the halfway line?

1007 And which Reading player suffered a serious knee injury in this match in January 2007?

1008 An ex-Reading striker scored twice against them in Sheffield Utd's 3-2 win at the MadStad on Easter Monday 2011. Who was he?

1009 Who did Reading purchase from the Blades in January 2013, just four days after Reading's 4-0 home defeat of his team in the FA Cup 4th Round?

1010 In April 2009, Reading lost 1-0 at home to Sheffield United, with the only goal being scored by a player they would later buy. Name him.

Quiz 102 - Reading & Sheffield Weds. *(Answers on page 139)*

1011 Who scored a hat-trick in Reading's 6-0 thrashing of Wednesday in September 2008?

1012 Which striker, who started his career at Slough Town, was signed by Reading from Sheffield Wednesday in March 2004 after a period on loan earlier that season?

1013 Reading met Wednesday in the FA Cup 4th Round at Hillsborough in January 2018. What was the final score in this match?

1014 In 2019/20, Wednesday had players sent off in both their matches against Reading. Name the two players red-carded.

1015 In February 2010, Reading beat Wednesday 5-0 at home. Which two players both scored a brace?

1016 Which Reading midfielder scored the last of his seven goals for the club in a 2-0 win at Hillsborough in December 2009?

1017 Which Reading youngster only made six starts for them, but later signed for Wednesday after a successful loan spell and scored 18 goals in 84 games for them before moving to the Premier League?

66

1018   Reading's first meeting with Wednesday came in the FA Cup at Elm Park in January 1929, with Reading beating the runaway leaders of the First Division. What was the score?

1019   Reading's first ever tier two match at the Madejski was against Sheffield Wednesday in August 2002. Who scored both their goals in a 2-1 win?

1020   Name the striker who joined Reading in August 2019, just three days after scoring against them for Wednesday.

Quiz 103 – 2003/04 Season *(Answers on page 140)*

1021   Reading opened the 2003/04 season with an away league match at Portman Road - and, almost inevitably, had a player sent off. In total, how many red cards did Reading players receive in this and their previous three trips to Ipswich?

1022   Alan Pardew's last match as Reading manager was at Selhurst Park in front of a crowd of 2,066. Who were the opposition, and why was the attendance so low?

1023   Which lanky striker made his first Reading start in the 2-1 home league win over Watford in November 2003? He'd previously made one substitute appearance, in the last match of 2001/02.

1024   Reading lost 3-0 to Burnley at Turf Moor in November 2003, facing a team that included a winger who had played for them on loan the previous season and another who would join them on loan later that season. Name them both.

1025   Reading lost three consecutive matches 3-0 in December 2003. Which team beat them in the third of these matches, played at the Madejski on Boxing Day?

1026   And which future Reading captain scored Wimbledon's third goal in this Boxing Day match?

1027   Which team knocked Reading out of the FA Cup in a 3rd Round replay in January 2004? The original tie had been a 3-3 draw in which two of Reading's goals were own goals!

1028   Which striker made his Reading debut when he came off the bench in the home 1-1 draw with Ipswich in January 2004?

1029   Reading beat Cardiff 3-2 at Ninian Park in March 2004. All three of their goals were scored by players who had signed for the club in the previous five months. Name them.

1030   Where did Reading lose 1-0 on the last day of the season to quash the slight chance they had of qualification for the play-offs?

Quiz 104 – Steve Coppell *(Answers on page 140)*

1031   With which club did Steve Coppell make his football league debut?

1032   What degree did he gain from the University of Liverpool whilst also playing professional football?

1033   To which team did Coppell lose his first FA Cup final, playing for Manchester United?

1034   What Manchester United record does Coppell hold - one unlikely ever to be beaten?

1035   For how many days was Coppell manager of Manchester City in October 1996?

1036   Which match was Coppell's first in charge of Reading?

1037   What award did Coppell win in May 2007?

1038   In May 2008, where did Reading fans congregate to publicly ask Coppell not to leave the club after relegation from the Premier League?

1039   Which midfielder, signed from Coventry, was Steve Coppell's last permanent signing for Reading?

1040   Which team in India did Coppell manage between June 2016 and July 2017?

Quiz 105 – 2004/05 Season *(Answers on page 141)*

1041   Which winger did Reading sign permanently from Leicester City in July 2004?

1042   After how many seconds of the 2004/05 league season did Reading concede their first goal?

1043   Which summer signing made his first Reading appearance in the 1-0 away defeat to West Ham in August 2004?

1044　Reading did the double over the Championship winners this season. Who were they?

1045　How did Reading's winter signing Les Ferdinand often travel to the training ground?

1046　Long-serving centre-back Ady Williams controversially left Reading in November 2004. Which club did he join?

1047　Which team did Reading beat 3-0 at the Madejski Stadium on Boxing Day 2004?

1048　How many league matches did Reading go without a league win after this Boxing Day victory?

1049　And who scored a hat-trick, and against which team, to bring this winless run to an end?

1050　Where did Reading play their last match of the season, watching the celebrations at the end as the home team was promoted to the Premier League?

Quiz 106 – The 106 Team *(Answers on page 141)*

1051　How many of the 106 point squad had previously played in the Premier League?

1052　Who was the most expensive acquisition of the 106 point team?

1053　Which member of the 106 point squad scored in the only match he started in 2005/06?

1054　How many of the 106 point squad joined Reading from Arsenal?

1055　How many members of the 106 point squad joined Reading in the summer of 2005?

1056　How many league goals did the members of the 106 squad score for the club in 2005/06?

1057　Which two members of the squad signed for Reading from Burnley?

1058　Which member of the 106 point squad made 38 league appearances in 2005/06 but only started three matches?

1059　How many players in total started league matches for Reading in 2005/06?

1060　Who was the only member of the 2005/06 squad to make ten or more league starts this season and not experience a league defeat?

Quiz 107 – **Reading & Southampton** *(Answers on page 142)*

1061   Reading first met Southampton in the FA Cup 2nd Round in 1891/92, and lost 7-0. Why did they still progress to the next round?

1062   Reading sensationally beat Saints 3-1 at St. Mary's in April 2012 to take a massive step towards securing the Championship title. Who scored Reading's first goal?

1063   And which player scored Southampton's equaliser in this Friday evening match?

1064   Which defender did Reading buy from Saints in August 2011? He would only make 14 appearances for them over the next two seasons.

1065   Which Southampton player joined Reading in December 1957 at the age of 28, and went on to score 27 goals in over 300 appearances over the next eight seasons?

1066   Which ex-Reading striker scored the fastest goal in Premier League history for Southampton in April 2019?

1067   In November 1995 Reading beat Southampton 2-1 at Elm Park to win through to the quarter-finals of the League Cup for the first time ever. Who scored their two goals?

1068   Who was Reading's manager for their only home Premier League meeting with Southampton?

1069   Which long-serving full-back joined Reading from Southampton in July 1982?

1070   What was Graeme Souness's main complaint about the FA Cup match between the clubs at Elm Park in January 1997, which would eventually lead to him being sent off, escorted away by stewards and charged by the FA?

Quiz 108 – **2005/06 Season** *(Answers on page 142)*

1071   Which Reading outfield player made 11 league starts in 2005/06 but failed to score a league goal?

1072   What was the name of the performance consultancy company engaged by Reading in the summer of 2005? Their participation played a major part in the team's success this season.

1073   Which player scored two of his five league goals of the 2005/06 season in consecutive away matches at the start of the season?

1074   Who scored the winning goal in Reading's thrilling 3-2 victory over Crystal Palace at the MadStad in September 2005?

1075   Where did Reading win 4-3 away in the league in February 2006?

1076   Which team did Reading draw 0-0 with in both home and away league matches in the 2005/06 season?

1077   Which Reading player scored just three league goals this season - all against the same opponents?

1078   What did Steve Coppell throw into the crowd at The Walker's Stadium?

1079   How many teams did Reading score five goals against in a league match this season?

1080   Kevin Doyle's equaliser at Leicester was scored on the last Saturday in March. What unusual horological record does this give Reading?

Quiz 109 – Behind the Scenes *(Answers on page 142)*

1081   Who was released as reserve team manager in the summer of 1999 as Tommy Burns disbanded the reserve team?

1082   Who was Reading's sales and marketing manager during the 2005/06 promotion-winning season?

1083   Who was Reading's general manager in the 1980s, said by some to be one of the reasons the TV Series "The Manageress" was filmed at Elm Park?

1084   What did Reading Football Supporters' Club become in March 2002?

1085   Who was Reading's kitman for over 16 years until his retirement in 2009?

1086   Which long-serving employee's testimonial match was the last match to be staged at Elm Park?

1087   Who was Reading's sporting director between April 2016 and September 2018?

1088   Name the former Reading managing director who was convicted in April 2007 of various offences of fraudulent trading which were committed whilst at Exeter City.

1089   Which physio, formerly with Reading for nine years but then with Chelsea, was publicly criticised in August 2015 by Jose Mourinho for attending to an injured Eden Hazard, meaning Hazard had to leave the pitch?

1090   Which former member of Reading's backroom staff was appointed Celtic's head of football operations in October 2019?

Quiz 110 – Reading & The Southwest *(Answers on page 143)*

1091   Which no-nonsense full-back joined Reading from Torquay in January 1999 for £100,000?

1092   Reading beat Plymouth 4-2 in the League Cup at Home Park in August 2019. Who scored two goals in the last three minutes to secure this victory?

1093   Who did Reading buy from Exeter in December 1990, in a £50,000 transfer personally funded by John Madejski - the first signing of his time at the club?

1094   What was unique about Reading's 6-4 victory over Exeter at St James Park in October 1993?

1095   Who scored both Reading's goals to defeat Plymouth 2-0 in their first home match back in the Championship in 2008/09?

1096   What was unusual about Reading's league match against Yeovil at the Madejski in March 2014?

1097   Who did Reading purchase from Plymouth in the summer of 1985? He later played a significant part in Reading's comeback from 3-0 down to beat Plymouth 4-3 in December 1985.

1098   Which Reading youngster joined Exeter in January 2016 after making just 36 Royals appearances?

1099   Who scored Plymouth's winning goal in the last minute of their win at the Madejski Stadium in August 2005?

1100   What happened at Plainmoor in August 2010 amidst Reading fans' celebrations for a winner in the last minute of extra time in their League Cup match with Torquay United?

1101   Who scored Reading's first ever Premier League goal, in August 2006?

1102   Which summer signing scored his first Reading goal in their first Premier League win away from home, at Sheffield United in September 2006?

1103   Which team did Reading meet in four separate matches this season?

1104   Which defender made his only Reading appearance in the League Cup win on penalties at home to Darlington in September 2006? He scored in the 87th minute to take the game into extra time.

1105   After not receiving any the previous season, how many red cards did Reading players receive in the 2006/07 season?

1106   Who was the Daily Mirror journalist who persistently blamed Stephen Hunt for "deliberately" injuring Chelsea's Petr Cech?

1107   Who scored twice in Reading's 6-0 demolition of West Ham at the Madejski on New Year's Day 2007?

1108   Which record signing, who joined the club in January 2007, only played in three matches for Reading before departing the club five months later?

1109   Who scored two late goals at The Reebok Stadium in April 2007 to turn around Reading's Premier League match against Bolton?

1110   How many teams did Reading do the league double over in this, their first Premier League season?

1111   Which goalkeeper made 22 appearances for Reading between 1994 and 1996 but never adequately replaced Shaka Hislop and didn't play league football after the age of 22?

1112   Which midfielder, signed by Tommy Burns from Luton for £500,000, came with a big reputation but failed to deliver on it? He made only one league appearance in his first three months at the club and just 18 in all.

1113   Which Ajax youngster conceded seven goals in his first two league matches for the Royals, the second from an Andy Legg back-pass? He then started only one more league game for Reading.

1114   Which Portuguese international won European trophies after leaving Reading, but only managed a total of 87 minutes on the pitch when he was with them?

1115   How many goals did on loan Chelsea 'keeper Nick Colgan concede in his five matches for Reading in 1998?

1116   Which player, who played 23 games for Reading in 2013/14 scoring two goals, quit football two years later, saying he was "fed up with all the stuff in the football world" and that he'd dedicate his life to rap music?

1117   Which big-money signing from Nantes in August 2007 contracted malaria while at the Africa Cup of Nations, and called Steve Coppell "stupid" when refusing to play for the reserve team? He made just eight Reading appearances.

1118   Which free transfer from Colorado Rapids made just two appearances for Reading in 2014/15, conceding a penalty in one of them, away at Blackpool?

1119   Name the Liberian who played 38 matches for Reading between 1998 and 2000, scoring three times, but never lived up to his potential and reputation.

1120   Which striker, hailed as "The Michael Owen of the North East", was signed by Tommy Burns on deadline day 1998 to score the goals needed to keep Reading up? In fact, he scored just one goal in 42 matches for Reading.

Quiz 113 – Reading & Stoke City *(Answers on page 144)*

1121   Who scored his first goal at the Madejski Stadium for Reading in a 3-3 draw with Stoke in August 2000?

1122   Which member of the 106 point team's last kick of the ball for Reading before departing on loan was to miss a penalty in the losing League Cup shoot-out with Stoke in September 2008?

1123   And which Reading player scored twice in normal time to get both of his team's goals in this 2-2 draw?

1124   In November 1998 Stoke became the first team to win an FA Cup match at the Madejski, with a 1-0 win. Who scored their goal?

1125   Which player signed from Stoke scored against them for Reading in April 2006?

1126   In December 2018 Reading drew 2-2 with Stoke at home in the Championship. Who scored their last-minute equaliser?

1127   Which full-back joined Reading from Stoke in July 2010?

1128   Which two members of the 106 point team joined Stoke after relegation in 2008?

1129   In March 1999 Reading beat Stoke 4-0 at The Britannia Stadium. Which striker, on loan from Sheffield Wednesday, scored Reading's first goal, on his Royals debut?

1130   Which experienced centre-back joined Reading from Stoke in January 2007?

Quiz 114 – 2007/08 Season *(Answers on page 144)*

1131   Against whom did Reading win their first Premier League match of this season?

1132   Against which team in August did injuries force Steve Coppell to make wholesale changes – ending up on the wrong end of a 3-0 scoreline?

1133   Whose last-minute winner at home to Sunderland in the Premier League in December 2007 was awarded by the assistant referee, who controversially ruled that the ball had crossed the line?

1134   Which Reading midfielder received a straight red card after just 29 minutes of the away match at West Ham on Boxing Day 2007?

1135   Who scored Tottenham's fifth goal in their 6-4 win over Reading in December 2007, despite clearly encroaching as Spurs took a penalty?

1136   Jimmy Kebe signed for Reading in January 2008. From which French club?

1137   Who scored twice in Reading's last home win of the season, a 2-1 defeat of Birmingham City in March 2008?

1138   Before beating Reading at The Madejski Stadium in April 2008, how many away league matches had Fulham played without registering a win?

1139   Against which team did Nicky Shorey make his full England debut, in June 2007?

1140   Who opened the scoring for Reading in the 16th minute of their last match of the season, away at Pride Park?

Quiz 115 – Elm Park (2) *(Answers on page 145)*

1141   In which year were floodlights installed at Elm Park?

1142   Which company sponsored the membership scheme for the South Bank in the 1980s?

1143   Which US rock band headlined the "Spring Thing" concert at Elm Park in April 1970?

1144   In what year were seven executive boxes first constructed in the main stand at Elm Park?

1145   What was the correct name for the South Bank?

1146   Who scored Reading's last competitive goal at Elm Park?

1147   To what figure was the capacity of Elm Park reduced for safety reasons only days before the start of the 1985/86 season?

1148   What pre-season mistake by Gordon Neate in August 1985 meant the postponement of two friendlies?

1149   What was the first Reading match at Elm Park to be televised live by Sky TV?

1150   In October 1984 George Best and Martin Peters played for Reading in a friendly at Elm Park. Which international team were the opposition?

Quiz 116 – Reading & Sunderland *(Answers on page 145)*

1151   Who scored twice for Reading in their 2-1 defeat of Sunderland at the Stadium of Light in April 2005?

1152   Who did Reading offload to Sunderland in the summer of 2007 - less than six months after they'd purchased him?

1153   Which goalkeeper, who joined Reading from Sunderland, was voted "MLS Goalkeeper of the Year" in October 2019?

1154 In which year was Reading's August Bank Holiday weekend match at Sunderland postponed due to a waterlogged pitch?

1155 Which player, later to join Reading, scored Sunderland's second goal in their 2-0 defeat of Reading at The Stadium of Light in September 2003?

1156 For which Reading player did Sunderland manager Roy Keane make an unsuccessful bid of £5M in January 2007?

1157 Who scored from the penalty spot for Reading as they drew 2-2 with Sunderland at the Madejski Stadium in April 2018?

1158 Who scored twice for Reading as they beat Sunderland 2-1 at home in the Premier League in February 2013?

1159 Two Reading managers have had successful playing careers at Sunderland. Name them both.

1160 Which signing from Sunderland was shown a straight red card on his first league start for Reading in September 2018?

Quiz 117 – 2008/09 Season *(Answers on page 145)*

1161 Who did Reading beat 2-1 in the League Cup in August 2008 - their only ever meeting with this team?

1162 In this League Cup match, which summer signing scored his first goal for the club after 89 minutes?

1163 Which Reading striker scored two hat-tricks in consecutive home matches in the late summer of 2008?

1164 Reading's first away league win of the season came at the end of September At which West Midlands team, and what was the score?

1165 In October 2008 Reading battered Burnley at Turf Moor but lost 1-0. Who was Burnley's goalkeeper who made a string of saves to keep them out?

1166 Reading's last home win of the season came at the end of January 2009, with a 1-0 win over Wolves. Which Wolves player scored a 3rd minute own goal and was sent off in injury time?

1167 Who scored for Ipswich against Reading in both home and away league matches?

1168 Brian Howard scored the only goal in a 1-0 away victory over Reading on Good Friday 2009. Who were the visitors to the Madejski?

1169   And with whom did Reading draw 2-2 on Easter Monday 2009?

1170   Reading lost their last match of the league campaign, at home to Birmingham, 2-1. Which Reading midfielder scored his second and last goal for the club in the 62nd minute of this match?

Quiz 118 – The Irish Connection *(Answers on page 146)*

1171   Who was manager of Cork City when Reading purchased Kevin Doyle and Shane Long in the summer of 2005?

1172   One of the "Magnificent Seven" purchased by Tommy Burns in March 1998 was Irish. Name him.

1173   Shane Long played at Croke Park in two All-Ireland Championship semi-finals. In which sport?

1174   In November 2019, which player who made 13 Reading appearances between 2000 and 2002 was appointed assistant manager of Cork City, the club where he started his career?

1175   Who won 17 international caps while a Reading player? This was a club record until surpassed by Kevin Doyle.

1176   Which ex-Reading player is third in the all-time list of most-capped Republic of Ireland players?

1177   Which ex-Reading full-back managed Cork Hibernians to both League of Ireland and FAI Cup victories in the 1970s?

1178   Which Irish international scored his first Premier League goal for Reading in the 2–2 draw with Newcastle in September 2012?

1179   Which defender made his first Republic of Ireland start against the Czech Republic in October 2006?

1180   Which Irish ex-Reading player was commissioned to write the book: *Unforgettable Fire - Past, Present, and Future - The Definitive Biography of U2* in 1985?

Quiz 119 – Reading & Swansea City *(Answers on page 146)*

1181   In September 2000 Reading beat Swansea 5-1 at the MadStad. Who scored a hat-trick for them in this match?

1182   Which striker, signed by Reading in August 2017, played 51 Premier League matches for Swansea over the previous three seasons, scoring one goal?

1183   Which Reading player was sent off after receiving two yellow cards at the Liberty Stadium in Reading's 2-0 league defeat there in January 2009?

1184   Who scored twice for Reading in their 4-0 home league defeat of Swansea in September 2008?

1185   Which Swansea player scored a hat-trick against Reading at Wembley in May 2011?

1186   Reading beat Swansea 3-1 away in March 1927 to create a record that would last for 88 years. What record?

1187   On New Year's Day 2019, Reading hosted Swansea at the Madejski Stadium in the Championship and lost 4-1. Who scored their single goal?

1188   Reading's last visit to The Vetch was in January 2005 for an FA Cup 3rd Round replay, which they won 1-0. Who grabbed the winner in the 95th minute?

1189   Which Swansea 'keeper's error gifted Reading a soft goal in their 2-2 Premier League draw at Swansea in October 2012?

1190   And who was Reading's goalkeeper in that 2-2 draw who made a series of exceptional saves to be hailed as man of the match?

Quiz 120 – 2009/10 Season *(Answers on page 147)*

1191   Who scored his first Reading goal in his team's 5-1 home League Cup defeat of Burton Albion in August 2009?

1192   Reading spent £2M to purchase centre-back Matt Mills in August 2009. From which team did they buy him?

1193   Where did Brendan Rodgers gain his first league win for Reading?

1194   Kevin Doyle left Reading to sign for Wolves in June 2009. What was the transfer fee?

1195   Brendan Rodgers was sacked in December after a home 1-1 draw with which team?

1196   Who scored the fastest ever goal by a Reading player, after just 9.5 seconds of his team's FA Cup 5th Round tie against West Brom at the Madejski in February 2010?

1197 And which Reading forward was sent off early in the second-half of this FA Cup tie against the Baggies?

1198 Gylfi Sigurðsson was awarded "Championship Player of the Month" for March 2010. How many goals did he score from the six matches he played this month?

1199 Which team did Reading beat 6-0 in their penultimate home league match of the season, in April 2010?

1200 Chelsea defender Ryan Bertrand spent a season-long loan with Reading, playing 51 matches in all competitions this season and scoring one goal. Who was it scored against?

Quiz 121 – Brian McDermott *(Answers on page 147)*

1201 Brian McDermott took temporary charge of Reading on a joint basis in October 2003 following the departure of Alan Pardew. Who did he share this role with?

1202 In what capacity did McDermott join Reading in September 2000, under Alan Pardew?

1203 With which team did McDermott serve his apprenticeship as a player?

1204 Who scored a last-minute equaliser and then immediately received a second yellow card in McDermott's first match in sole charge of Reading?

1205 Who took over as caretaker manager for two weeks when McDermott was sacked by Anton Zingarevich in March 2013?

1206 With which club did McDermott first gain managerial experience, joining them as a player in 1996 and being promoted to player-manager the following year?

1207 Who did McDermott replace as manager of Leeds United in April 2013?

1208 Which prospective owner of Leeds "sacked" McDermott in early 2014, only for the club to reinstate him a few days later?

1209 The same team were the opposition for both McDermott's first and last matches in his second spell at Reading in 2015/16. Which team?

1210 The defeat of which team gave McDermott his first win as Reading manager, in January 2010?

Quiz 122 – Reading & The Rest (1) *(Answers on page 147)*

1211   Which young player did Alan Pardew sign from Leyton Orient in February 2001 for an initial £25,000?

1212   Reading knocked Gillingham out of the League Cup at the Madejski Stadium in August 2017. Who scored both their goals in this 2-0 victory?

1213   Which two Reading players scored their first FA Cup goals for the team in the 2-2 draw away at Blackpool in January 2020?

1214   In 2001/02, Reading beat Port Vale 2-0 both home and away in the league, with one player scoring all four goals. Name him.

1215   Who played for Crawley Town in their home FA Cup 3rd Round defeat to Reading in January 2013 - and signed for the Royals eight days later?

1216   Who scored two goals for Reading as they beat Walsall 4-0 in the FA Cup 4th Round at the MadStad in January 2016?

1217   Dean Morgan joined Reading in November 2003. From which club?

1218   Which long-serving Reading player scored the last of his 52 Reading goals in a home match against Southend in February 1997?

1219   Which ground did Reading play at for the first time ever in their last away league match of the 2016/17 season?

1220   In 1976, Reading were promoted from Division Four alongside Lincoln, who set a new Football League record for points in a season, with 74. How many points would Reading's 106 in 2005/06 add up to in the era of two points for a win?

Quiz 123 – 2010/11 Season *(Answers on page 148)*

1221   Reading lost their first league match of the season, a 2-1 home defeat. To whom?

1222   Who did Reading sign from Carlisle in August 2010?

1223   Gylfi Sigurðsson left Reading at the end of August 2010. Who did he sign for?

1224 Which Norwich striker was sent off just before half-time in Reading's 3-3 draw with the Canaries at the Madejski in November?

1225 Reading scored four goals in a Championship game four times in this season - and five on one occasion. Which team did they beat 5-2 at the MadStad in March 2011?

1226 Which striker, who'd scored 13 goals for his previous club in the first half of the season, got his first Reading goal in his second match for them, at Cardiff in the Championship in February 2011?

1227 How many consecutive league matches did Reading win from the beginning of March 2011?

1228 Reading's promotion hopes took a major dent on Easter Monday 2011 when former striker Darius Henderson scored twice against them. For which team?

1229 Away to which team did Reading draw 0-0 to secure their place in the play-offs?

1230 Who scored an outstanding solo goal to round off Reading's away play-off win at the Cardiff City Stadium in May 2011?

Quiz 124 – League Cup (2) *(Answers on page 148)*

1231 Which team thrashed Reading 6-0 in the 2013/14 League Cup?

1232 Which Division One team did Reading knock out of the League Cup in 1978/79?

1233 Who scored Reading's first-half goal as they lost 2-1 to Everton in the 3rd Round at the MadStad in September 2015?

1234 What was the final score in the League Cup 2nd Round match when Reading beat West Ham Utd on September 11th 2001?

1235 Who scored Reading's single goal in the 2-1 Quarter-Final defeat at Elland Road in January 1996?

1236 Which Wolves player scored an own goal to help Reading beat Wolves 4-2 at Elm Park in the 1997/98 3rd Round tie?

1237 And which Reading midfielder scored Reading's second goal in that tie, a 25-yard cracker?

1238   Who knocked Reading out of the League Cup in November 2005?

1239   Reading beat Burton Albion 5-1 in the League Cup 1st Round in August 2009. Name the two players who each scored two goals.

1240   Who were sponsors of the League Cup when Maurice Evans led Oxford United to victory in 1986?

Quiz 125 – Reading & The Rest (2) *(Answers on page 148)*

1241   Reading lost to Northampton Town on penalties in the League Cup at the MadStad in August 2010 after a 3-3 draw. Who scored two goals for Reading - but also the 120th-minute equaliser for Northampton at the wrong end?

1242   In February 2016, Reading beat Charlton 4-3 at The Valley. Who scored a hat-trick for Charlton in this match, and who scored Reading's winner in the 90th minute?

1243   Which league team have Reading only played in the FA Cup, with four matches between the clubs, including matches in both 2010/11 and 2011/12?

1244   In February 2004, Rotherham comprehensively beat Reading 5-1 in the league at Millmoor. Which ex-Reading striker scored their third goal in this game?

1245   For which player did Reading agree a transfer fee with Crewe in January 1996? Reading could not meet his wage demands and he joined Leicester City instead.

1246   At which ground in Cheshire have Reading played just one match, a 2-1 Division Two defeat in September 1998?

1247   From which club did Reading purchase Adam Le Fondre for £300,000 in August 2011?

1248   Which ex-Reading player was voted Blackpool's Player of the Season in 1982/83?

1249   In April 1999 Reading lost 2-1 at Gillingham in the league. Which former Reading player scored the Gills' second goal?

1250   Which two league teams on the Lancashire coast have Reading never met in a competitive match?

Quiz 126 – 2011/12 Season *(Answers on page 149)*

1251 Which player signed from QPR at the end of August and was ever-present in the heart of Reading's defence for the rest of the Championship season?

1252 How many penalties were Reading awarded in their home Championship match with Barnsley in August 2011?

1253 At which stadium was there a late postponement of Reading's away match in February 2012, due to a frozen pitch?

1254 In which crucial match did Reading concede a goal after just eight minutes but recovered to win 4-2?

1255 Before which home match was it announced by Sir John Madejski that he intended selling the club to a consortium known as "Thames Sports Investments"?

1256 How many matches did Reading win in the second half of the Championship season?

1257 Against which team did Reading clinch the 2011/12 Championship title?

1258 Which Reading player was sent off just before half-time in that final home league match?

1259 Who did Reading lose to in the last match of the season?

1260 Who was the first player Reading signed after winning promotion?

Quiz 127 – Play-offs (3) *(Answers on page 149)*

1261 Which of Reading's six away play-off semi-finals had the biggest attendance?

1262 Which Swansea player was playing in the second of three consecutive Championship play-off finals when he faced Reading?

1263 Which Wigan player scored from a free-kick to give the visitors a second leg play-off lead at the Madejski in 2001?

1264 Which teams met at Wembley just two days before Reading and Swansea in 2011?

1265 Who scored from the penalty spot to give Burnley a 1-0 lead at Turf Moor in May 2009?

1266	Which Reading striker scored twice at Prenton Park in the first leg of the 1995 play-off semi-finals?
1267	Whose shot hit the Swansea post in 2011 with the score at 3-2 to Swansea?
1268	Who scored the only goal in the 2003 play-off semi-final second leg at the Madejski Stadium?
1269	Who did Paul McShane foul to receive a straight red card at Craven Cottage in 2017?
1270	How many red cards have Reading players received in total across their 16 play-off matches?

Quiz 128 – Reading & Tottenham *(Answers on page 150)*

1271	Which home-grown star joined Spurs from Reading in 1953 for a fee equivalent to £15,000?
1272	Which Spurs player scored the last goal at The Madejski Stadium in Reading's first Premier League spell?
1273	What was the embarrassing score when Reading visited White Hart Lane at the start of the 1930/31 Division Two campaign?
1274	Which former England Under-18 team captain did Reading purchase from Spurs in February 1996 for £700,000?
1275	In the 2012/13 Premier League season Spurs beat Reading by the same score in both home and away matches. What score?
1276	Which Reading player scored his first Premier League goal at the Madejski in November 2006 in Reading's win over Spurs?
1277	Who scored four goals against Reading in Tottenham's 6-4 win at White Hart Lane in December 2007?
1278	Seven days later, that player scored twice more as Spurs and Reading drew 2-2 in an FA Cup 3rd Round match at White Hart Lane. Who scored two goals for Reading in this game?
1279	And which Spurs player was sent off after 83 minutes of that cup tie, just four minutes after coming on as a substitute?
1280	Which lifelong Spurs fan scored twice against them for Reading at White Hart Lane in December 2007?

Quiz 129 – 2012/13 Season *(Answers on page 150)*

1281   Which striker did Reading sign on a free transfer from Fulham in July 2012?

1282   Who scored his only Premier League goal for Reading in their 4-2 defeat at Stamford Bridge in August 2012?

1283   How many goals did Arsenal score against Reading this season?

1284   Which Reading player's girlfriend took to Twitter in September 2012 to complain about him being dropped from the team?

1285   Reading won just one Premier League match before Christmas 2012. Who did they beat in it?

1286   Adam Le Fondre twice came off the bench in Premier League matches in January and scored two quick goals to change the game. Against which opponents?

1287   Eamonn Dolan took charge of just one match as Reading's caretaker manager. Where was it?

1288   And where was Nigel Adkins's first match as Reading manager, two weeks later?

1289   Reading won just one of their last 13 Premier League matches this season. Who was it against?

1290   Only one player featured in all 38 of Reading's Premier League matches, but his only goal was in the FA Cup. Who?

Quiz 130 – Transfer Fees *(Answers on page 150)*

1291   In the summer of 1995 Reading's record transfer fee received was broken three times in five weeks. Who was the third of these expensive departures?

1292   Which goalkeeper did Reading break their transfer record to buy for £300,000 in September 1995?

1293   And which player did they more than double this record to purchase from Tottenham in February 1996?

1294   Emerse Fae signed as a supposed replacement for Steve Sidwell in August 2007 for a new record fee. How much did Reading pay Nantes for him?

1295   Which player signed for Reading in the summer of 1997 for £800,000, a new club record - and which club did he join from?

1296   The sale of which player in August 2010 set a new record for the highest transfer fee received by Reading - and who was the player whose sale set the previous record?

1297   In July 2004, Reading broke their transfer record to purchase which US international?

1298   Which England international did Reading break their transfer record to sign from Spurs for a reported £2,750 in 1947?

1299   Reading broke their transfer record to purchase George Puşcaş in August 2019. From which club and how much did they pay?

1300   Greg Halford was a record signing, purchased for £2.5M and sold six months later at a slight profit. From whom did Reading purchase him?

Quiz 131 – Reading & Watford *(Answers on page 151)*

1301   In September 2008 Reading were wrongly awarded a "ghost goal" at Watford by referee Stuart Attwell - to which Watford player was this accredited as an own goal?

1302   Which defender did Reading pay Watford £2.5M to purchase in July 2012?

1303   Reading drew 3-3 with Watford at the Madejski in August 2013. Which Reading midfielder scored two of his team's goals?

1304   Name the Reading assistant manager who first joined the club in the summer of 2006, after a three-year spell developing Watford's youth and reserve teams.

1305   Reading beat Watford 1-0 in the Championship at Vicarage Road in January 2014, with a goal scored after just five minutes. Who scored it?

1306   Peter Castle became Reading's youngest ever player with a substitute appearance at Vicarage Road. In the last match of which season?

1307   Which player, who scored 26 goals in 91 games for Reading, signed from Watford for £250,000 in January 1995?

1308   In the 2005/06 Championship season, both matches between Reading and Watford had an identical score. What was it?

1309   Which player made 214 appearances for Watford before joining Reading in November 1979? He retired from football due to a hip problem just 14 months later.

1310   The Hornets finished third in the Championship in 2005/06 but were promoted via the play-offs, eight weeks and a day later than Reading's promotion was confirmed. How many points behind Reading were they in finishing third?

Quiz 132 – 2013/14 Season *(Answers on page 151)*

1311   USA international Danny Williams joined Reading in June 2013. From which club did he sign?

1312   Who scored for Ipswich against Reading in their first Championship match of the season, in August 2013?

1313   After playing League Cup matches in previous seasons, which Reading youngster finally made his league debut for Reading in the 3-1 win away at Derby in September 2013?

1314   In November, Reading lost 5-2 to Sheffield Wednesday. Which ex-Royal scored the Owls' second goal in this match?

1315   Reading humiliated their ex-captain Matt Mills by trouncing his team 7-1 when they visited the Madejski in the Championship in January 2014. Which team was he with?

1316   Which former Reading Player of the Season scored QPR's goal in their 3-1 Championship defeat to Reading at the Loftus Road in February 2014?

1317   In April 2014, Reading's Under-21 team won the inaugural Under-21 Premier League Cup. Against which team did they overcome a 3-2 first leg deficit by winning the home leg 2-0?

1318   In May 2014, Reading hurriedly sold Adam Le Fondre to Cardiff for an estimated £2.5M. What forced this sale upon them?

1319   Which three members of "Thames Sports Investments" were ousted from the board of Reading FC in June 2014?

1320   Reading fans embarrassed themselves with an abortive pitch invasion after the final home match of the season, against Burnley. Which team's last-minute winner kept Reading out of the play-offs and sent those fans gingerly slinking off the pitch?

Quiz 133 – Welsh Royals *(Answers on page 151)*

1321   Which Reading player holds the record as most capped player for Wales?

1322   Which Welsh team beat Reading 3-0 in the first match of the 19989/99 season?

1323   Name the Reading manager who gained 41 caps for Wales.

1324   How many matches against Welsh teams did Reading play in the 2010/11 season?

1325   Which Welsh player once held the world record for the longest throw-in, with a distance of 44.6 metres?

1326   Which ex-Reading striker was nominated alongside Lionel Messi for the 2016 FIFA Puskás Award for "most beautiful" goal of the year for a goal scored for Wales?

1327   In 1995 two Reading team-mates played together for Wales in a home match against Moldova. Name them both.

1328   Which defender played 16 times for Wales before joining Reading in July 1992?

1329   Three of the "Death Row Five" sidelined by Tommy Burns were Welsh. Name them.

1330   What was significant about Reading's last away league match at Newport County?

Quiz 134 – Reading & West Brom *(Answers on page 152)*

1331   Which Reading player scored a hat-trick to beat West Brom in an FA Cup 3rd Round replay in January 2006?

1332   And who scored West Brom's two goals in reply in this match?

1333   Which Reading striker did West Brom pay Reading £6.5M to sign in August 2011?

1334   Which young goalkeeper failed to hold down a place in three years at Reading and joined West Brom in July 2018?

1335   In the Premier League match between Reading and West Brom at the Madejski in January 2013, which Baggies player scored twice to give the visitors a 2-0 lead?

1336   Which former WBA player scored his first goal for Reading in their 3-1 FA Cup 5th Round win over his old club at The Madejski in February 2016?

1337   And how was Baggies defender Chris Brunt injured shortly after the end of this match?

1338   Who scored a spectacular extra time winner at The Hawthorns in February 2010 to see Reading into the 6th Round of the FA Cup with a 3-2 win?

1339   Which full-back did Reading sign on a free transfer from West Brom in July 2012?

1340   What did Baggies fans dress up as for their visit to the Madejski for Reading's last match of the 2003/04 season, to honour their Player of the Season, Thomas Gaardsøe?

Quiz 135 – 2014/15 Season *(Answers on page 152)*

1341   Which USA Under-18 international did Reading sign in June 2014?

1342   Which player arrived on loan at Reading at the start of September, and scored twice on his Reading debut?

1343   In September, Michael Hector scored his first goal for Reading, in a 3-3 home Championship draw. Against which team?

1344   After which heavy Championship defeat was Nigel Adkins sacked as Reading manager?

1345   Steve Clarke's first win, in his third match as Reading boss, was a 2-1 home Championship win over one of the teams promoted at the end of this season. Which team?

1346   Which player did Reading sign on a free transfer in February 2015? He played for them in four FA Cup matches, scoring the winning goal in the first of them.

1347   Reading beat Bradford City in the FA Cup quarter-final in March 2015. At which Premier League team had Bradford won 4-2 in the 4th Round?

1348   In March 2015, why were Reading fined £30,000 by the Football League?

1349   The FA Cup quarter-final replay with Bradford City was interrupted by a rotund pitch-invader. What did he do in the Reading penalty area - several times?

1350   Reading stunned Derby in the last match of the season with a 3-0 away win which ended Derby's play-off hopes. In this match, which Reading 'keeper saved a penalty - and from which Derby player?

Quiz 136 – Loan Players *(Answers on page 153)*

1351   Who did Reading sign on loan from Liverpool in January 2019?

1352   Who did Reading take on loan from Stoke City in March 2009 until the end of the season?

1353   Which loanee from West Ham made one Championship appearance for Reading in 2005/06 – in which he took the free-kick that set up Brynjar Gunnarsson's 89th-minute winner?

1354   Promising youngster Aaron Kuhl spent three months on loan at a Scottish club in 2015, but after his return never fulfilled his potential. Which Scottish club?

1355   Which on loan striker scored the first of his two goals in ten games for Reading in a 1-0 home Championship win over Charlton?

1356   Ryan Bertrand spent a season-long loan with Reading in 2009/10. From which Premier League club?

1357   Defender Zurab Khizanishvili spent a season-long loan with Reading in 2010/11. From which club?

1358   In January 2015, young midfielder Aaron Tshibola moved on loan to a team that was struggling at the bottom of League Two and helped them avoid relegation out of the Football League. Which club?

1359   In September 2014, Reading loaned out Royston Drenthe to another Championship club for four months. Which club?

1360   Which goalkeeper spent two months on loan at Leeds between November 2011 and January 2012?

Quiz 137 – **Reading & West Ham** *(Answers on page 153)*

1361   Which Australian signed permanently for Reading from West Ham in March 1997 after a successful loan spell?

1362   Who was the former West Ham centre-back who played 26 times for Reading between November 2014 and April 2016?

1363   How many goals in total have been scored in FA and League Cup matches between Reading and West Ham since 1920?

1364   Every Reading fan should know this - what was the final score in the Premier League meeting between Reading and West Ham at the Madejski Stadium on 1st January 2007?

1365   And who was West Ham's manager for this classic New Year's Day match?

1366   Which player joined Reading in the summer of 1995 but in just his third Reading match suffered a suffered a depressed skull fracture via the elbow of Portsmouth's Jon Gittens?

1367   Reading won their first Premier League match at the Boleyn Ground, in October 2006, by a single goal. Who scored it after just two minutes?

1368   Who scored a Premier League hat-trick against Reading in West Ham's 4-2 home win in May 2013?

1369   In March 2012, Reading visited the Boleyn for a top-of-the-table Championship clash. What was the final score in this?

1370   In December 2011, Reading beat West ham 3-0 at the Madejski in a match where the visitors ended up with nine men. What did Jimmy Kebe do that made Jack Collison see red and flatten him after the ball had gone?

Quiz 138 – **2015/16 Season** *(Answers on page 153)*

1371   Which future Reading captain signed for them from Hull City in July 2015?

1372   Which player did Reading sell to Chelsea in September - and then immediately take back on loan until the end of the season?

1373   Orlando Sa scored a hat-trick in a 5-1 home Championship in September 2015. Who were the opponents?

1374   In December, why was Steve Clarke "relieved of his duties" as Reading manager?

1375   Who took over as Reading's caretaker manager?

1376   Brian McDermott returned as manager in December 2015. Which match was his first in charge, and what was the score?

1377   In Jan. 2016 Reading signed two players from Premier League clubs. Name them both and the clubs they signed from.

1378   Reading beat Huddersfield 5-2 at home in the FA Cup 4th Round in January 2016. Who scored three Reading second-half goals?

1379   In March, which Reading player was sent off after 85 minutes of the 2-0 home FA Cup quarter-final defeat to Crystal Palace?

1380   Who was Reading's top scorer this season, despite not having been at the club since January?

Quiz 139 – FA Cup (2) *(Answers on page 154)*

1381   On which neutral ground was Reading's 1927 FA Cup semi-final played?

1382   Which non-League club forced a 1-1 home draw with Reading in the 3rd Round amidst torrential rain in January 1998?

1383   Who scored Reading's three goals to take them to Wembley in 2015?

1384   Which young player scored Reading's goal as they drew 1-1 with Manchester City at Maine Road in January 1993?

1385   Which player's only Reading goal was the winner in a 5th-round match at Pride Park in February 2015?

1386   Which amateur club did Reading beat 8-3 in the FA Cup 1st Round in 1935-36, their highest FA Cup victory excluding qualifying rounds?

1387   Which ex-Reading youngster faced Reading twice for West Brom in the 2009/10 FA Cup?

1388   At which Yorkshire team did Reading lose 4-3 in the 3rd Round in 1985?

1389   Whose brace for Arsenal settled the 2014/15 FA Cup semi-final?

1390   How many times have Reading reached the quarter-finals of the FA Cup?

Quiz 140 – Reading & Wigan *(Answers on page 154)*

1391   When did Reading and Wigan first meet in the Football League?

1392   Which Wigan player scored against Reading both home and away in the 2006/07 Premier League matches?

1393   In the last match of the 2004/05 season, which future Reading signing scored against them in Wigan's 3-1 win to gain promotion?

1394   Who scored all three of Reading's goals in the 3-1 Championship win at the DW Stadium in November 2019?

1395   Which Reading player was sent off at the Madejski in February 2013 as Reading lost to Wigan 3-0 in the Premier League?

1396   How many goals in total did Reading and Wigan share in their four matches in 2000/2001?

1397   Which player did Reading sign from Wigan on a free transfer in December 1999? He made just one Royals appearance, in a Football League Trophy win over Orient that same month.

1398   What was the score in Reading's Premier League game with Wigan in April 2008, their penultimate away match of that relegation season?

1399   Which Reading player scored his only Reading goal in his team's last visit to Springfield Park, a 4-1 defeat in April 1999?

1400   Which Wigan player scored an own goal in his team's 3-2 home Premier League win over Reading in November 2012?

Quiz 141 – 2016/17 Season *(Answers on page 155)*

1401 Which Reading shareholder fronted the press announcement of Jaap Stam as Reading manager in July 2016?

1402 Which Dutch player did Reading sign from FC Dordrecht in July 2016?

1403 Which Reading player scored on his debut in the first match of the 2016/17 season, a 1-0 home Championship win over Preston?

1404 Who scored both Arsenal goals as they knocked Reading out of the League Cup in October 2016?

1405 Which team beat Reading 5-0 in the Championship in December 2016?

1406 Manchester United beat Reading in the 3rd Round of the FA Cup at Old Trafford in January What record did Wayne Rooney equal when he scored their first goal?

1407 Which young player made 12 Reading appearances in the 2016/17 season, scoring two goals?

1408 At which club did Reading concede six first-half goals, as well as scoring one of their own, in April 2017?

1409 Reading got their first ever win at Villa Park with a 3-1 Championship victory on Easter Saturday 2017. Who scored two of their three goals?

1410 In which competition did a Reading Under-23 team participate this season, for the first time?

Quiz 142 – Managers (3) *(Answers on page 155)*

1411 Which Reading manager twice played as an emergency goalkeeper for the team in 1963/64?

1412 Which Reading manager, sacked in February 1969, returned to the club as secretary in 1977?

1413 Which ex-Reading manager went on to manage the Scotland national team on a permanent basis?

1414 Which Reading manager's only previous managerial experience was at Barnet?

1415 Alan Pardew left Reading to become manager of which club?

1416   Which club did José Gomes manage before joining Reading?

1417   Which four Reading players were initially appointed joint-caretaker managers following the departure of Mark McGhee?

1418   Who won only seven out of his 30 matches as Reading manager?

1419   Which Reading manager was named Sunderland's "Player of the Century" in 1979?

1420   Which Reading manager was replaced in the role by another whose title-winning hopes had been ruined by Reading's 3-1 away win less than a year earlier? And who replaced him?

Quiz 143 – Reading & Wimbledon *(Answers on page 155)*

1421   Which striker, on loan at Reading for the 2014/15 season, started his career with Wimbledon?

1422   Which former Reading player scored Wimbledon's most celebrated goal?

1423   Which young Reading defender spent all of the 2018/19 season on loan at AFC Wimbledon?

1424   Who scored two goals as Reading beat Wimbledon 3-0 at Selhurst Park in Alan Pardew's last match as manager in August 2003?

1425   And which two players in the losing Wimbledon team that day later signed for Reading?

1426   Which future Reading coach made 340 league appearances for Wimbledon between 1979 and 1988?

1427   Which ex-Reading coach spent ten months as manager of AFC Wimbledon from December 2018?

1428   Reading's last visit to Plough Lane was in October 1981. What was the score in that match?

1429   Which ex-Wimbledon player, together with Jack Black, sent a motivational video message to the 106 point team from Hollywood in 2005/06?

1430   On 14th September 2002, Reading lost 1-0 to Wimbledon at the Madejski in Division One. Who did AFC Wimbledon beat 2-0 at Kingsmeadow on the same day?

Quiz 144 – 2017/18 Season *(Answers on page 156)*

1431 Which promising young player was allowed to join Charlton in June 2017, after making just one Royals substitute appearance?

1432 Which Reading defender received a red card in the first match of the 2017/18 season, an away defeat to QPR?

1433 Two players were signed by Reading from Wolves in the summer of 2017. Name them both.

1434 Reading won consecutive league matches just twice this season - which two teams, located close to each other, did they beat within four days of each other in October and November 2017?

1435 Which summer signing scored the first of his five Reading goals in a 3-1 home League Cup win over Millwall in August 2017?

1436 Who joined Reading on loan from Aston Villa in January 2018?

1437 Reading only had one Championship win between 2nd December 2017 and 30th March 2018, a run of 18 matches. Who was it against?

1438 And who scored a rare goal for Reading in this match?

1439 What was the score and opposition in Reading's last home match of the season in April 2018?

1440 Reading flirted with relegation all season. Who did they play in their last match in May 2018, earning a 0-0 draw that ensured their survival?

Quiz 145 –Madejski Stadium (2) *(Answers on page 156)*

1441 In 2000, which team did New Zealand beat 84-10 at the Madejski in the Rugby League World Cup?

1442 Which global megastar played a concert at the Madejski in May 2005?

1443 Which radio presenter was a guest at the opening ceremony of the Madejski Stadium, making the on-pitch announcements?

1444 Who scored the first hat-trick at the Madejski Stadium?

1445   And who scored the first hat-trick for Reading at the Madejski Stadium?

1446   In June 2013, Jessie J, JLS, Lawson, Amelia Lily and Union J were among the acts that performed at the Madejski in a summer concert. What was this event billed as?

1447   What architectural feature behind the East Stand at the Madejski Stadium only survived a few matches before it was deemed unsafe and removed in 1998?

1448   Which team scored the first away goal at the Madejski, in September 1998?

1449   What family-orientated event did Reading host at the Madejski Stadium in May 2016?

1450   Which two Reading heroes are celebrated by blue plaques on the wall of the Madejski Stadium?

Quiz 146 – Reading & Wolves *(Answers on page 157)*

1451   Ian Porterfield's first permanent signing was a player from Wolves. Name him.

1452   In the league draw with Wolves at Elm Park in December 1997, which Reading defender was sent off in a case of "mistaken identity" - and who was he mistaken for?

1453   On Boxing Day 2005, Reading travelled to Wolves and won the Championship match 2-0. Who scored their goals?

1454   Which Wolves goalie scored an own goal after just four minutes of Reading's visit to Molineux in September 2008?

1455   In September 2002, who scored a remarkable long-range "freak" goal at Molineux to give Reading a 1-0 league win there?

1456   Which defender, purchased from Wolves on October 2003, was Steve Coppell's first signing for Reading?

1457   Which Reading striker scored his only goal for the club against Wolves in a 3-1 away defeat in April 1998?

1458   Which two members of the 106-team joined Wolves in the summer of 2009?

1459   And who did Reading sign from Wolves in July 2006 in preparation for their first Premier League season?

1460   Reading met Wolves with Mark McGhee as manager five times. How many of those matches did they win?

Quiz 147 – 2018/19 Season *(Answers on page 157)*

1461   Which team beat Reading in the Championship at the Madejski in August 2018, despite facing financial problems and under threat of a winding-up order?

1462   Which striker signed for Reading in July 2018, but left on loan just six months later after only starting six matches?

1463   What was Reading's first Championship win of the 2018/19 season, achieved in their seventh match?

1464   Reading's biggest win this season was a 3-0 home Championship victory in September 2018. Against which team?

1465   Paul Clement was sacked as Reading manager in December 2018. Who took over as caretaker manager from him?

1466   Who left Reading just one day after Clement's sacking, after less than four months as sporting director?

1467   In January 2019, David Edwards left Reading. Which club did he join?

1468   In the same month, Lewis Baker arrived on loan for the rest of the season. From which club?

1469   In March 2019, Mark Bowen arrived at Reading. What was his role upon his arrival?

1470   What was the score in Reading's last two home Championship matches of the season?

Quiz 148 – Transfer Trails (4) *(Answers on page 157)*

Name the Reading player from their transfer history. The number of league appearances made for Reading is shown in brackets.

1471   Reading (72) > Portsmouth > Nottingham Forest > Manchester United > Nottingham Forest > Swindon Town (loan) > Instant-Dict (loan) > Grimsby Town > Aldershot Town

1472   Reading (104) > Newcastle United > West Ham United > Portsmouth > West Ham United > FC Dallas

1473   Watford > Reading (29) > Crystal Palace > Watford

1474   Greenock Morton > Newcastle United > Aberdeen > Hamburg > Celtic > Newcastle United > IK Brage > Reading (45)

1475   Cardiff City > Tottenham Hotspur > Nottingham Forest (loan) > Nottingham Forest > Reading (273)

1476   Southampton > Chelsea > Fulham (loan) > Manchester City > West Ham United (loan) > Sunderland (loan) > Brighton (loan) > Reading (12)

1477   Manchester United > Blackpool (loan) > Birmingham City (loan) > Celtic (loan) (0) > Reading (104)

1478   Reading (219) > Millwall > Southampton > Oxford United > Woking

1479   Reading (393) > Mikkelin Palloilijat (loan) > Chelsea (loan) > Southampton (loan) > Wolves > Millwall > Slough Town

1480   St Patrick's Athletic > Cork City > Reading (154) > Wolves > Queens Park Rangers (loan) > Crystal Palace (loan) > Colorado Rapids

Quiz 149 – Reading & Yorkshire Clubs *(Answers on page 158)*

1481   From which Yorkshire club did Reading acquire Andy Yiadom in July 2018?

1482   Which on loan Reading player helped Huddersfield win the 2012 Football League One play-off final?

1483   In October 2010 Reading beat Doncaster 4-3 at home in The Championship. Which Reading player scored their first, against his old team?

1484   Huddersfield beat Reading 6-1 in February 1982. Who scored Reading's single goal?

1485   Which Bradford player was sent off in March 2015 as Reading progressed to the semi-finals of the FA Cup?

1486   Who left Reading to join Huddersfield in August 1993 after making 216 league appearances in the previous six and a half years?

1487   Which Reading player scored and received a red card in his team's 2-1 win at Barnsley in September 2016?

1488   Reading's last away match of 2013/14 was a 3-1 win at Doncaster. Who scored two late goals to secure this win?

1489   Which Reading defender was sent off at Valley Parade in a 2-1 defeat to Bradford City in April 2004?

1490   In August 2014, which player was spotted at the Madejski Stadium watching Reading, the club he would join two days later, lose 2-1 to the club he then played for?

Quiz 150 – Royals Records *(Answers on page 158)*

1491   Against whom was Reading's largest ever win, 10-2, achieved in September 1946?
1492   How long did Steve Death go without conceding a goal in 1979?
1493   How many consecutive league games did Reading win at the start of the 1985/86 season, a Football League record?
1494   Who has made the most appearances for Reading, with a total of 603?
1495   What is Reading's highest-scoring defeat - and to whom?
1496   Who holds the record for most league goals in a season for Reading?
1497   Where did Peter Castle, Reading's youngest ever player, make his only Reading appearance?
1498   What unfortunate records do Reading hold in both the Premier League and the League Cup?
1499   What was the highest ever attendance at Elm Park, to watch a 1-0 FA Cup 5th Round win over Brentford in February 1927?
1500   Trevor Senior has scored the most goals for Reading. How many?

Answers

Quiz 1 – Origins

1   St Mary's Reading Rooms, Gun Street.
2   Although Joseph Sydenham called the meeting at which the club was founded and became its secretary, James Simonds was its first chairman.
3   21st February 1872.
4   King's Meadow Recreation Ground, v. Reading Grammar School FC.
5   2-2-6.
6   Windsor Home Park, 20th November 1872.
7   Edward Haygarth, in Reading's 3rd match, a 13-a-side game against Reading Grammar School.
8   So the Reading team could catch a GWR train back to Reading.
9   Reading Hornets. Many Hornets players had previously played for Reading.
10   The FA Cup.

Quiz 2 – Transfer Trails (1)

11   Darren Caskey.
12   Gylfi Sigurðsson.
13   Martin Hicks.
14   Nicky Shorey.
15   Steve Death.
16   Adam Federici.
17   Liam Moore.
18   Robin Friday.
19   Lawrie Sanchez.
20   Martin Butler.

Quiz 3 – Reading & Arsenal

21   Alexander Hleb.
22   They were both scored by Reading players – Stuart Morgan and John Harley.
23   Theo Walcott.
24   Fever Pitch, by Nick Hornby.
25   4-0 to Arsenal, at the MadStad in October 2006.
26   Martin Keown.

27   *Adam Federici.*
28   *Graham Stack.*
29   *Uncle and nephew.*
30   *Trevor Senior.*

Quiz 4 – The Southern League Years
31   *Swindon Town.*
32   *Turning professional.*
33   *Champions.*
34   *Phil Bach.*
35   *2nd, in 1902/03, 1904/05 and 1914/15.*
36   *8-0.*
37   *AC Milan.*
38   *Allen Foster.*
39   *Bradford Park Avenue.*
40   *Baseball.*

Quiz 5 – The Madejski Stadium (1)
41   *Luton Town, beaten 3-0 in August 1998.*
42   *Richmond FC.*
43   *£1 – although he then had to pay to decontaminate the land, previously used for storing hazardous waste.*
44   *Grant Brebner.*
45   *Everton.*
46   *Shooters.*
47   *36,900.*
48   *Bury.*
49   *Red Hot Chili Peppers.*
50   *Nathan Tyson.*

Quiz 6 – Reading & Aston Villa
51   *John Carew.*
52   *Ibrahima Sonko.*
53   *Ulises de la Cruz.*
54   *Sam Baldock.*
55   *Nelson Oliveira.*
56   *Nicky Shorey & Steve Sidwell.*

57   Dion Dublin.
58   2-1 to Villa - due to a late Terry Bell own goal.
59   Aaron Tshibola.
60   Steve Sidwell.

Quiz 7 – Reading in the 1920s
61   Jimmy Lofthouse.
62   Gillingham, who beat them 2-1.
63   Joe Bailey.
64   Manager.
65   George Murray.
66   Alf Messer.
67   Reading 7, Brentford 1.
68   Frank Richardson.
69   Villa Park.
70   Bill Johnstone.

Quiz 8 – Play-offs (1)
71   Swansea in 2011, watched by 86,581. The 2017 final attracted 76,682.
72   Tranmere Rovers.
73   Tony Rougier.
74   Barry Hunter.
75   Nicky Forster.
76   Stephen Hunt, Glen Little & Dave Kitson.
77   Their shoes.
78   Neil Swarbrick.
79   Steve Beddow. He was joined on the walk by John Madejski, Mike Lewis and Uri Geller.
80   Martin Butler.

Quiz 9 – Reading & Brum/Coventry
81   Michael Morrison.
82   1-1.
83   Demarai Gray.
84   Glenn Murray.
85   10.38pm.

86   *Ady Williams.*

87   *Nicky Forster.*

88   *Matt Miazga (51), Yakou Méïté (56) and Pelé (87).*

89   *Tony McPhee.*

90   *Leroy Lita.*

Quiz 10 – Reading in the 1930s

91   *Reading Football Supporters' Club.*

92   *Arthur Bacon.*

93   *Fulham.*

94   *Jack Palethorpe.*

95   *Frank Newton, signed in Sept. 1933.*

96   *Tommy Tait.*

97   *QPR.*

98   *A tin of Huntley & Palmers biscuits.*

99   *Blue and white hoops.*

100   *Joe Edelston.*

Quiz 11 – Cup upsets

101   *Guildford City, who won 1-0.*

102   *Five. Only Bradford were in Division Two.*

103   *Leeds Utd.*

104   *Bishop's Stortford, who won an FA Cup 1st Round match in 1982.*

105   *West Bromwich Albion.*

106   *Pat Earles.*

107   *York City.*

108   *Everton.*

109   *West Ham.*

110   *Wealdstone.*

Quiz 12 – Reading & Blackburn Rovers

111   *David Bentley.*

112   *Three - 3-1 at home and 3-2 away.*

113   *Jason Roberts.*

114   *Jón Daði Böðvarsson.*

115   *Seol Ki-Hyeon.*

116   *Marek Matejovsky.*

117   *Marcus Hahnemann.*

118   *Kevin Doyle.*

119   *4-0 - with goals from Canoville, Wood, Senior & Bremner.*

120   *Hope Akpan & Danny Guthrie.*

Quiz 13 – World War II Royals

121   *Half price entry for members of the armed forces.*

122   *The London War Cup.*

123   *Brentford.*

124   *White Hart Lane.*

125   *Matt Busby.*

126   *8-2.*

127   *Ted Drake.*

128   *44.*

129   *Southampton.*

130   *Frank Ibbortson.*

Quiz 14 – Top Scorers

131   *Ron Blackman, with 158 league goals.*

132   *Tony McPhee.*

133   *Kerry Dixon, who scored 26 goals in 1982/83.*

134   *Stockport County.*

135   *41 goals.*

136   *Arthur Bacon.*

137   *Ian Harte.*

138   *Jimmy Quinn.*

139   *Crystal Palace.*

140   *21 - 7-4 at Portsmouth and 6-4 at Spurs in 2007/08.*

Quiz 15 – Reading & Bournemouth

141   *Jack Stacey.*

142   *Jimmy Quinn in 1992/93 and Yann Kermorgant in 2016/17.*

143   *3-3 draw.*

144   *Reading would have played Bournemouth in the play-off semi-final instead of Wigan.*

145   *Jamie Cureton and Martin Butler.*

146   *Jermain Defoe.*

147 Ian Harte.

148 Barry Hunter.

149 Peter Grant and Chris Casper.

150 Adam Federici.

Quiz 16 – Post-War Biscuitmen

151 Maurice Edelston. Although he did play in Division Three (South) matches in 1939/40 but these matches were later expunged from records.

152 Tony McPhee.

153 A Tannoy system.

154 They threw snowballs at him.

155 Ron Blackman.

156 Layer Road, Colchester Utd.

157 Ted Drake.

158 Jimmy Hill.

159 Bryn Allen.

160 Tommy Lawton.

Quiz 17 – Goalkeepers

161 Fulham.

162 Nick Colgan.

163 Shaka Hislop.

164 Stewart Henderson.

165 Peter van der Kwaak.

166 Alex McCarthy.

167 John Turner.

168 Portuguese.

169 Cardiff City.

170 Steve Death.

Quiz 18 – Reading & Brentford

171 Carl Asaba.

172 The London War Cup.

173 The 77th.

174 Sam Sodje.

175 Michael Hector.

176 Tony Rougier & John Salako.

177   *Ibrahima Sonko and Stephen Hunt.*
178   *33,042.*
179   *Jón Daði Böðvarsson.*
180   *Wally Downes.*

Quiz 19 – Reading in the 1950s

181   *Manchester Utd.*
182   *Ron Blackman.*
183   *Plymouth Argyle.*
184   *Chelsea.*
185   *Maurice Evans.*
186   *Colchester Utd.*
187   *Divisions Three (North & South) were restructured, so any teams finishing in the bottom half started the next season in Division Four.*
188   *Gordon Banks.*
189   *Hospital Radio Reading.*
190   *Tommy Dixon.*

Quiz 20 – League Cup (1)

191   *Eric Nixon, on loan from Tranmere.*
192   *Maidstone Utd.*
193   *Craig Hignett.*
194   *George Cain ("The butcher of Bootle").*
195   *Wolves.*
196   *Peterborough Utd.*
197   *Chelsea.*
198   *Colin Gordon.*
199   *Mark McGhee.*
200   *Bristol Rovers, in October 1960.*

Quiz 21 – Reading & Brighton.

201   *Four times - 2001/02, 2002/03, 2004/05, 2005/06.*
202   *Oliver Norwood.*
203   *Dave Kitson.*
204   *Ian Harte.*
205   *Tyler Blackett.*
206   *Four times - the initial 1st Round match plus three replays.*

207   *Dick Knight.*
208   *Sam Baldock.*
209   *Paul Brooker. Ivar Ingimarsson also played for Brighton in this match.*
210   *Glen Little and Dave Kitson.*

Quiz 22 – Reading in the 1960s

211   *Peter Bonetti and Peter Osgood.*
212   *The League Cup.*
213   *Roots Hall, Southend.*
214   *Friday evening matches. These lasted until 1966, when they were abandoned as only Saturday matches received a share of revenue from the football pools.*
215   *Arthur Wilkie. As no substitutes were allowed, he came back on after injury and played as a winger.*
216   *Fulham.*
217   *Manchester City, in January 1968.*
218   *Peter Silvester.*
219   *Four.*
220   *Gordon Neate, who worked as groundsman until 2009.*

Quiz 23 – Managers (1)

221   *Roy Bentley.*
222   *Brian McDermott in his second spell (161 days), Brendan Rodgers (194 days), Paul Clement (258 days), José Gomes (290 days) & Steve Clarke (353 days).*
223   *"Terry the Taxi".*
224   *Maurice Evans.*
225   *Jaap Stam. Paul Clement also won one as Real Madrid's assistant manager.*
226   *Ian Porterfield, for Sunderland in 1973 or Ted Drake for Arsenal in 1936.*
227   *Harry Johnson, manager for 2616 days. Joe Edelston had a longer term as manager, but this spanned World War 2.*
228   *Martin Kuhl.*
229   *Andrew "Angus" Wylie.*
230   *Alan Pardew.*

Quiz 24 – Reading & Bristol City & Rovers

231   *Simon Church.*
232   *Jamie Cureton and Jason Roberts.*
233   *Trevor Senior.*
234   *Jeff Hopkins.*
235   *Leroy Lita.*
236   *Dean Horrix.*
237   *Yann Kermorgant.*
238   *Scott Murray.*
239   *Mathieu Manset.*
240   *Terry Cooper.*

Quiz 25 – Reading in the 1970s

241   *The Watney Cup, a pre-season competition for the previous season's highest-scoring teams.*
242   *The closure of Huntley and Palmers biscuit factory.*
243   *Jack Mansell.*
244   *None. They were relegated back the following season.*
245   *Bob Lenarduzzi.*
246   *Andy Alleyne.*
247   *John Murray.*
248   *Tommy Youlden's free-kick went the wrong side of the post, but the referee and linesman awarded it as a goal.*
249   *5-0.*
250   *Graham Taylor.*

Quiz 26 – Sendings Off

251   *Keith Gillespie.*
252   *Dave Kitson.*
253   *Andy Bernal and Andy Legg.*
254   *None.*
255   *Jack Collison.*
256   *John Swift.*
257   *Ivar Ingimarsson.*
258   *Alan Maybury.*
259   *Sam Sodje. He was booked twice in 11 minutes after coming off the bench.*

260   Paul McShane.

Quiz 27 – Reading & Burnley & Preston
261   Glen Little & John Oster.
262   Matt Miazga. This was Mark Bowen's first match in charge.
263   Leroy Lita.
264   Eight, in an 8-1 win.
265   18-0.
266   Steve Sidwell & John Salako.
267   Nicky Forster.
268   Andre Bikey.
269   They warmed up in the same half as Preston.
270   Mike Conroy.

Quiz 28 – 1978/79 Season
271   Steve Hetzke.
272   Southampton. They drew 0-0 but lost the replay 2-0.
273   His false leg fell off, and was carried separately by another police officer!
274   Full-backs Mark White & Gary Peters; centre-backs Paul Bennett & Martin Hicks.
275   Gillingham.
276   John Alexander.
277   Pat Earles (15), Ollie Kearns (11), Richie Bowman & Mike Kearney (10 each).
278   George Shipley.
279   Northampton Town.
280   Rochdale.

Quiz 29 – Royals in Europe
281   Daniel Carriço.
282   Sevilla FC, of Spain.
283   Gylfi Sigurðsson and Danny Williams, who were teammates at Hoffenheim and started six games together.
284   Sweden.
285   Neil Webb.
286   Italy.
287   Les Ferdinand.

288   Bayern Munich.
289   1 point - they had a better goal difference than Bolton, who finished in seventh place.
290   Royston Drenthe.

Quiz 30 – Reading & Cambridgeshire

291   £150,000.
292   6-0 to Peterborough.
293   Tony Rougier.
294   Chris Gunter.
295   James Harper.
296   13 times.
297   Bryan Carnaby.
298   Ron Atkinson.
299   Martin Butler.
300   Gylfi Sigurðsson.

Quiz 31 – 1979/80 Season

301   Fulham.
302   Stewart Henderson.
303   Hugh Cheetham.
304   Barnsley.
305   He sent them down a coal mine to show them what "real work" was like.
306   Neil Webb.
307   Richie Bowman.
308   Steve Wood.
309   Provide urine samples for drug testing.
310   Steve Death.

Quiz 32 – FA Cup (1)

311   Manchester United.
312   1877.
313   Chelsea.
314   Wealdstone, who won 2-1.
315   Billy Sharp, who scored an extra time winner for Sheffield Utd in March 2020.

316   Brentford.
317   Garath McCleary.
318   Micah Richards.
319   Gylfi Sigurðsson.
320   Brynjar Gunnarsson.

Quiz 33 – Reading & Cardiff City
321   Andre Bikey, sent off in a 2-2 draw in November 2008.
322   Five - 5-1 at home and 5-2 away.
323   Cameron Jerome.
324   Sean Morrison.
325   Shane Long.
326   Jobi McAnuff.
327   1998.
328   Dean Morgan.
329   George Puscas.
330   Adam Federici.

Quiz 34 – 1980/81 Season
331   Mike Kearney.
332   Stuart Beavon.
333   Jerry Williams.
334   Kerry Dixon.
335   None.
336   £1.60.
337   Luton Town.
338   Martin Hicks.
339   Ron Fearon.
340   Neil Webb.

Quiz 35 – Reading at Wembley
341   Five times.
342   One - the 1994/95 play-off final vs. Bolton.
343   Steve Sidwell, who came on as a Chelsea substitute in the 2007/08 Community Shield.
344   Assistant manager Nigel Gibbs, in the 2011 Swansea play-off final.
345   Michael Gilkes, to equalise in the Simod Cup Final.

346 *1-3. 1-2 from the Bolton match and 0-1 from the Arsenal match.*

347 *The Rumbelows Sprint Challenge.*

348 *Third - winning £1,000. The race was won by Swansea's John Williams.*

349 *Lawrie Sanchez.*

350 *Ten.*

Quiz 36 – Reading & Chelsea

351 *Paul Canoville, who had been forced to retire through injury.*

352 *Michael Essien.*

353 *Michael Hector.*

354 *Tony McPhee.*

355 *Khalifa Cisse.*

356 *Pavel Pogrebnyak and Danny Guthrie.*

357 *Seven. He also came off the bench eight times.*

358 *Matt Miazga.*

359 *Adam Le Fondre.*

360 *Three - Petr Cech and Carlo Cudicini went off injured, and John Terry completed the game in goal.*

Quiz 37 – 1981/82 Season

361 *Neil Webb. Kerry Dixon scored 12 goals.*

362 *League rules were changed to award three points for a win.*

363 *The Football League Group Cup, introduced as a replacement for the Anglo-Scottish Cup.*

364 *Huddersfield Town.*

365 *Steve Death.*

366 *He was representing England in the World Youth Cup in Australia.*

367 *Gary Heale. He was sold to Sparta Rotterdam the following summer.*

368 *Colin Court.*

369 *They were both own goals conceded by the 'keepers.*

370 *Exeter City. They lost 4-3 at St James Park in November 1981 and won 4-0 at Elm Park in March 1982.*

Quiz 38 – Robin Friday

371 *Hayes. He'd impressed Charlie Hurley in their FA Cup games against Reading in December 1972.*

372   *Northampton Town, in January 1974.*
373   *Tranmere Rovers.*
374   *Clive Thomas.*
375   *By kissing a policeman.*
376   *He'd travelled on the train without buying a ticket - he only had a platform ticket.*
377   *Super Furry Animals.*
378   *46.*
379   *"Player of the Millennium".*
380   *Mark Lawrenson.*

Quiz 39 – Reading & Crystal Palace

381   *10-2.*
382   *Simon Osborn.*
383   *Kevin Doyle.*
384   *Four. June 1984 to May 1993; June 1995 to Feb 1996; Feb 1997 to March 1998 & Jan 1999 to August 2000.*
385   *Ibrahima Sonko.*
386   *Adrian Mariappa & Jimmy Kebe.*
387   *Lloyd Owusu.*
388   *Jake Cooper.*
389   *Ray Houghton.*
390   *"Tracksuit from Matalan".*

Quiz 40 – 1982/83 Season

391   *Portsmouth.*
392   *The rule punishing a "professional foul" with a red card.*
393   *Four.*
394   *1,943.*
395   *Deep Purple.*
396   *That he had agreed to sell the club to Robert Maxwell who would be merging Reading and Oxford United.*
397   *Oxford United.*
398   *32, which included 26 from 35 league games.*
399   *Phil Stant.*
400   *Wrexham. They did win, 1-0, but none of the other results happened and they were relegated by one point.*

Quiz 41 – "Thames Valley Royals"

401   *A coffin - signifying the death of Reading Football Club.*

402   *Robert Maxwell.*

403   *Roger Smee.*

404   *Didcot, although this was only ever suggested. No firm proposals were ever made.*

405   *Roy Tranter.*

406   *2-1 to Reading, through an 82nd minute own goal and an 88th minute Kerry Dixon penalty.*

407   *The Daily Mirror. He was later discovered to have illegally borrowed hundreds of millions of pounds from his companies' pension funds to rescue his companies.*

408   *Derby County.*

409   *June. Waller and other Reading directors who supported it had resigned and returned unissued shares to the board, effectively defeating the merger, in May.*

410   *A blue plaque on the wall outside the ticket office at the Madejski Stadium.*

Quiz 42 – Reading & Derby County

411   *Nick Blackman. He scored one goal for them.*

412   *Seven. They won 4-0.*

413   *Stephen Warnock.*

414   *Tomasz Cywka.*

415   *1-0. Trevor Senior scored after 63 minutes.*

416   *Charlie Adam.*

417   *Tariqe Fosu.*

418   *Kwesi Appiah.*

419   *Modou Barrow.*

420   *Shane Long.*

Quiz 43 – 1983/84 season

421   *6-2, against Stockport County.*

422   *Four.*

423   *The shirts were light blue and white "Argentina" shirts.*

424   *Ian Branfoot.*

425   *Mansfield, who beat them 2-0 at Field Mill in Mar 1984.*

426   *Nine.*

427   *Gillingham.*

428   *Mark White.*

429   *York City & Doncaster Rovers.*

430   *Away at Hartlepool. Reading drew 3-3.*

Quiz 44 – Sponsors

431   *The Reading Chronicle.*

432   *Bukta.*

433   *Gowrings, a Ford main dealer in Bracknell and Wokingham.*

434   *An IT distribution company based in Theale.*

435   *Puma.*

436   *Kyocera Mita.*

437   *Radio 210, who sponsored Reading's shirts in 1983/84. Football League rules at the time said the only numbers allowed on shirts were the player's number on the back.*

438   *Waitrose, between 2008 and 2015.*

439   *HAT Painting.*

440   *Courage.*

Quiz 45 – Reading & Everton

441   *Matt Mills.*

442   *Ross Barkley and Gerard Deulofeu.*

443   *Swansea City.*

444   *Hal Robson-Kanu.*

445   *Ten. The match was their 11th of the season, on November 17th 2012.*

446   *Adam Le Fondre.*

447   *Marcus Hahnemann.*

448   *Stephen Hunt.*

449   *Three - two Championship matches plus the League Cup match at Wolves. He conceded six goals in them.*

450   *Andrew Johnson.*

Quiz 46 – 1984/85 Season

451   *Michael Gilkes.*

452   *Seven executive boxes.*

453   *Barry Town, who they beat 2-1 away, and Bognor, who they beat 6-2.*

454 Dean Horrix.

455 George Best.

456 Gary Peters.

457 Bradford City. This was the last match at Valley Parade before the tragic fire that killed 56 supporters just one week later.

458 Ian Juryeff.

459 Eight.

460 By finishing top scorer in Division One with Chelsea, he'd been top scorer in Divisions Three, Two and One in consecutive seasons.

Quiz 47 – Royals in Management

461 Keith Curle.

462 Colchester Utd.

463 David Beckham, loaned to Preston North End during Peters's spell in charge.

464 Lawrie Sanchez.

465 Alan Pardew.

466 Shrewsbury Town.

467 Jimmy Wheeler.

468 Trevor Senior.

469 Chris Casper, in 2005. His playing career was ended by Cardiff's Richard Carpenter in the match on Boxing Day 1999.

470 Doncaster Rovers. The club's chairman at this time, Ken Richardson, was found guilty of conspiracy to commit arson after hiring three men to torch Belle Vue's main stand.

Quiz 48 – Reading & Fulham

471 Liam Rosenior.

472 Danny Williams.

473 Fulham 2, Reading 4.

474 Hal Robson-Kanu.

475 Ian Branfoot.

476 Yann Kermorgant.

477 Tomas Kalas.

478 Tomas Kalas, red-carded for a foul on Mo Barrow.

479 Neil Smith.

480 Gary Peters.

Quiz 49 – 1985/86 Season

481　*Identity cards - although this scheme was never fully implemented.*

482　*Colin Baillie.*

483　*Spurs.*

484　*Somerton Park, home of Newport County. The "new" Newport County, reformed in 1989, play at Rodney Parade.*

485　*Stuart Beavon, in a 2-0 win for Reading.*

486　*Trevor Senior. The other goals were scored by Dean Horrix with a penalty and Kevin Bremner.*

487　*Brentford.*

488　*Andy Rogers.*

489　*Derby County.*

490　*Frank Richardson, the only surviving member of that team from 60 years earlier.*

Quiz 50 – Transfer Trails (2)

491　*Kerry Dixon.*

492　*Martin Keown.*

493　*Ronnie Blackman.*

494　*Trevor Senior.*

495　*Garath McCleary.*

496　*Ady Williams.*

497　*Stephen Hunt.*

498　*Shane Long.*

499　*Andy Hughes.*

500　*Ibrahima Sonko.*

Quiz 51 – Reading & Humberside

501　*Paul McShane.*

502　*John Alexander.*

503　*Marcus Williams.*

504　*Glen Little.*

505　*Glen Little.*

506　*Nigel Adkins.*

507　*John O'Shea.*

508　*Lee Nogan.*

509　*Jake Taylor.*

510   *Stephen Hunt.*

Quiz 52 – 1986/87 Season
511   *Paul Canoville.*
512   *Twerton Park, also the home of Bath City.*
513   *Ron Futcher. Hicks later won a legal action against Futcher.*
514   *Barnsley.*
515   *Bob Hazell.*
516   *Gary Westwood.*
517   *Jerry Williams.*
518   *Trevor Senior.*
519   *Derby County.*
520   *Colin Baillie.*

Quiz 53 – Famous Fans
521   *John Arlott.*
522   *Bill Oddie.*
523   *Uri Geller.*
524   *Jo Sale.*
525   *David Brent, from "The Office".*
526   *Natalie Dormer.*
527   *Waldemar Januszczak.*
528   *The Hoosiers.*
529   *Kate Winslet.*
530   *Chris Tarrant.*

Quiz 54 – Reading & Ipswich Town
531   *Nelson Oliveira.*
532   *Andy Bernal.*
533   *Bobby Mihaylov.*
534   *Five. Bobby Mihaylov in 1996/97, Andy Bernal & Andy Legg in 1997/98, Adrian Viveash in 2002/03 and Nicky Shorey in 2003/04.*
535   *Nicky Forster.*
536   *Ivar Ingimarsson.*

537   *Five. Robert Fleck, Stuart Gray, Scott Howie, Patrick Kelly and Jim McIntyre all started the match, while the other two (Paul Brayson and Jimmy Crawford) both came off the bench during the match.*

538   *1-1.*

539   *They overtook Sheffield United to go top of the Championship table - a position they maintained all season.*

540   *Orlando Sa.*

Quiz 55 – 1987/88 season

541   *Millwall.*

542   *Málaga. Reading lost 3-0.*

543   *Kerry Dixon. They beat his Chelsea team 5-4 on aggregate.*

544   *Keith Curle.*

545   *Southampton, for whom Matt Le Tissier scored the only goal.*

546   *Colin Gordon.*

547   *Bradford City. They lost 1-0 away in a League Cup 4th Round replay after a goalless home tie, but won 2-1 in the Simod Cup.*

548   *Oxford Utd.*

549   *Just ten.*

550   *Hull City. It turned out to be irrelevant, as Sheffield Utd won so Reading would have been relegated even if they'd beaten Hull.*

Quiz 56 – The Simod Cup

551   *An Italian sports footwear manufacturer.*

552   *QPR - this was played on the plastic pitch at Loftus Road.*

553   *Linden Jones.*

554   *Stuart Beavon.*

555   *Dean Horrix.*

556   *Michael Gilkes.*

557   *Coventry's Steve Ogrizovic.*

558   *Gary Peters and Jerry Williams.*

559   *Luton's Mick Harford.*

560   *Steve Francis, who won it with Chelsea as they beat Manchester City 5–4 in 1986.*

Quiz 57 – Reading & Leeds

561   *Simon Church.*
562   *Brian McDermott.*
563   *Trevor Morley. The other goals were scored by Carl Asaba and Martin Williams.*
564   *Carlisle United.*
565   *Jem Karacan. He was the victim of heavy challenges from Danny Pugh and Michael Brown.*
566   *Neil Warnock.*
567   *Shaun Allaway. He made one substitute appearance for Leeds.*
568   *Jimmy Kebe.*
569   *Dylan Kerr.*
570   *Royston Drenthe.*

Quiz 58 – 1988/89 Season

571   *Keith Curle. He was sold for a fee of £500,000.*
572   *Wimbledon.*
573   *Billy Whitehurst.*
574   *Middlesbrough.*
575   *He broke his arm.*
576   *Gary Phillips.*
577   *Due to the lack of gates in the fences at Elm Park, following the Hillsborough disaster.*
578   *Seven.*
579   *Chesterfield, away at Saltergate.*
580   *4-2 to Reading, including two Stuart Beavon penalties.*

Quiz 59 – Elm Park (1)

581   *Willie Cunningham.*
582   *The General Strike of 1926 meant that work to build it didn't start until the middle of June*
583   *Bradford City.*
584   *Joe Louis, "The Brown Bomber."*
585   *The Royals Rendezvous.*
586   *Great Britain.*
587   *1949.*
588   *"The Manageress."*

589   *Racing Club de Paris.*
590   *1957.*

Quiz 60 – Reading & Leicester City

591   *Steve Moran.*
592   *Ricky Newman.*
593   *Paul Brooker.*
594   *Chris Makin.*
595   *1-1 draws in both matches. Andy Bernal scored Reading's goal in the away match, and Stuart Lovell scored from the penalty spot at home.*
596   *Liam Moore.*
597   *Alex Pearce, in the 16th minute.*
598   *Mikele Leigertwood. He only played two more matches for the club after this match.*
599   *Scott Taylor.*
600   *Saturday 25th March 2006 - the date of the club's first ever promotion to the Premier League.*

Quiz 61 – 1989/90 season

601   *Welling. After drawing 0-0 twice and 1-1 once, Reading won 2-1 with Steve Moran scoring both goals.*
602   *Shrewsbury Town.*
603   *Newcastle Utd.*
604   *The 4-1 away defeat to Orient on 21st October 1989.*
605   *Lew Chatterley.*
606   *Ian Porterfield.*
607   *Sunderland.*
608   *Ten - three against Bristol Rovers, four against Welling, one against Sunderland and two against Newcastle.*
609   *Dean Horrix, who had recently joined Bristol City from Millwall.*
610   *Linden Jones.*

Quiz 62 – Chairmen and Owners

611   *Bill Lee.*
612   *Frank Waller.*
613   *Adwest Engineering Ltd.*
614   *Roger Smee.*

615   Anton Zingarevich.

616   Renhe Commercial Holdings Company.

617   1990, in November.

618   £306,000. However, he also took on the club's debts of around £1M.

619   Lady Sasima Srivikorn.

620   He had been defeated in the "Thames Valley Royals" scheme.

Quiz 63 – Reading & Liverpool

621   The League Cup, in October 2006. Having never played each other throughout their entire existences, they also met in the Premier League just ten days later.

622   4-3 to Liverpool. After being 3-0 and then 4-1 down, Reading scored twice late on to make the score respectable.

623   Fernando Torres.

624   Tiago Ilori.

625   Dirk van Kuyt.

626   Alex McCarthy.

627   Ryan Bertrand.

628   Brynjar Gunnarsson.

629   Emiliano Insua.

630   Marek Matejovsky.

Quiz 64 – 1990/91 Season

631   They helped with stewarding of England fans during Italia 90.

632   Craig Maskell.

633   It was set at £250,000 by a Football League tribunal, considerably more than Reading expected.

634   Ron Blackman.

635   Steve Death.

636   Robin Friday.

637   Stuart Lovell.

638   It was the first match of the John Madejski era, following his rescue of the club the previous month.

639   He was facing a charge for drink driving, and had also failed to disclose to the club offers for players made by other clubs which he had declined.

640   Alex Ferguson.

Quiz 65 – Play-offs (2)

641   *Home to Wolves in 2003, 24,060.*

642   *Zurab Khizanishvili.*

643   *Huddersfield's Michael Hefele.*

644   *Andre Bikey, away at Burnley in 2009.*

645   *Nathan Tyson.*

646   *Nine, but in that time he created one goal, won a penalty and scored from the rebound of it.*

647   *Peter Shilton.*

648   *Jay Tabb.*

649   *Michael Gilkes.*

650   *Swansea in 2011.*

Quiz 66 – Reading & Local Rivals

651   *Sammy Igoe.*

652   *Ollie Kearns.*

653   *Darius Henderson.*

654   *Tony Rougier.*

655   *Neil Smillie.*

656   *Trevor Morley.*

657   *Scott Howie.*

658   *Shaun Goater in the 62nd minute and Andy Hughes in the 77th.*

659   *Sean Morrison.*

660   *6-2.*

Quiz 67 – 1991/92 Season

661   *Steve Moran.*

662   *Slough Town. After a 3-3 draw at Wexham Park, they won the replay at Elm Park 2-1.*

663   *Kevin Dillon.*

664   *David Lee.*

665   *Jim Leighton.*

666   *Steve Archibald.*

667   *200 career goals.*

668   *Torquay United.*

669   *Michael Gilkes, who came third in the final of the Rumbelows Sprint Challenge.*

670   Trevor Senior, in the 3-2 home defeat of Wigan in May 1992, the last match of the season.

Quiz 68 – Premier League Royals

671   Five. Reading, Chelsea, Aston Villa, Fulham and Stoke.
672   Neil Webb. He also made one appearance for Manchester United in that season.
673   Nathan Ake.
674   Gylfi Sigurðsson, playing for Swansea in January 2012, and setting up Danny Graham to score.
675   Reading, with 19 goals in two seasons. He scored 18in three seasons with Wolves, and none in a short loan spell with Crystal Palace.
676   Manchester City.
677   Michail Antonio.
678   Shaka Hislop, who played for Newcastle, West Ham (twice) and Portsmouth.
679   Simon Osborn, who joined from Crystal Palace and left to join QPR.
680   Simon Cox.

Quiz 69 – Reading & Luton Town

681   Graeme Murty.
682   They were scored by brothers. Noel Hunt after 10 minutes and Stephen Hunt four minutes later.
683   Les Sealey.
684   Sean Evers.
685   Win at home - in a 3-2 victory.
686   Kevin Doyle.
687   Dean Morgan.
688   Jamie Cureton.
689   Jack Stacey.
690   Reading 3, Luton 0.

Quiz 70 – 1992/93 Season

691   Manchester United. The score was 1-1 with a Reading trialist John Clayton scoring their goal.
692   Maidstone United, their 1st Round opponents, went bust a few days before the tie was due to be played.
693   Jeff Hopkins.

694 *Bury.*

695 *James Lambert.*

696 *AS Monaco, managed at the time by Arsene Wenger.*

697 *Scott Taylor.*

698 *Wigan in September 1992 and Preston in February 1993.*

699 *Jimmy Quinn.*

700 *The signing, Shaka Hislop, had graduated from Howard University with a degree in Mechanical Engineering, including an internship with NASA.*

Quiz 71 – Sir John Madejski

701 *Richard John Hurst.*

702 *Stoke-on-Trent.*

703 *Thames Valley Trader (later renamed Thames Valley Auto Trader).*

704 *Hurst Publishing.*

705 *The Victoria and Albert Museum.*

706 *2009.*

707 *Luxury Cars.*

708 *Cilla Black.*

709 *"Thames Sports Investments."*

710 *Burlington House, part of the Royal Academy of Arts.*

Quiz 72 – Reading & Manchester City

711 *4-0.*

712 *Reading won 3-0, with goals from Lee Hodges, Ray Houghton and Carl Asaba.*

713 *Shaun Goater, signed for £500,000.*

714 *Gareth Barry.*

715 *Leroy Lita.*

716 *Aaron Kuhl.*

717 *The 6th Round (quarter-finals).*

718 *1-0 to Reading, through a goal by Ivar Ingimarsson.*

719 *Lee Nogan.*

720 *Wayne Bridge.*

Quiz 73 – 1993/94 Season

721 *Steve Richardson.*

722   Dylan Kerr, signed for £75,000.

723   Huddersfield Town.

724   6-4 to Reading.

725   Stuart Lovell, Jimmy Quinn and Scott Taylor. Exeter players Ronnie Jepson and Mickey Ross both scored two each for the home team.

726   Uwe Hartenberger.

727   Seven times - at home to Barnet and Hartlepool and away at Bradford, Exeter (where they scored six), Port Vale, Hartlepool and Blackpool.

728   40 goals - 35 of them in the league.

729   Brighton, in the last home match of the season. Once other results were known they were also confirmed as league champions.

730   Ady Williams, who played for Wales against Estonia, in Tallinn. He qualified through his father, who was born in Wales.

Quiz 74 – Transfer Trails (3)

731   Terry Hurlock.

732   Stuart Lovell.

733   Alex Pearce.

734   Marc McNulty.

735   Graeme Murty.

736   John Salako.

737   Jobi McAnuff.

738   Mick Gooding.

739   Stuart Beavon.

740   Steve Sidwell.

Quiz 75 – Reading & Man United

741   Sam Sodje.

742   In January 1927, on the way to the FA Cup semi-final.

743   Michael Duberry.

744   Grant Brebner.

745   Marcus Rashford.

746   Kevin Doyle, who scored a 49th minute penalty, and Cristiano Ronaldo, who equalised in the 74th minute.

747   Luke Chadwick. He started the first match, and then came on as a late substitute in the second leg at the Madejski.

748   Tyler Blackett.

749   3-0 to Manchester United, through goals from Gabriel Heinze (3rd minute), Louis Saha (5th) and Ole Solskjaer (7th).

750   Chris Casper.

Quiz 76 – 1994/95 Season

751   Celtic.

752   Daley Thompson.

753   Due to a fire alarm in the main stand - it later transpired that a Reading fan's pipe was smouldering in his pocket!

754   Wolves. They won 4-2 through goals from Simon Osborn, Jimmy Quinn and two from Michael Gilkes.

755   Lee Nogan.

756   Paul Holsgrove.

757   Swindon Town.

758   Bolton. Reading's goals were scored by Stuart Lovell and Lee Nogan.

759   Charlton Athletic - a 2-1 win with goals from Lee Nogan and Ady Williams.

760   Stuart Lovell, with 14 goals in all competitions, ahead of Lee Nogan with 12.

Quiz 77 – Assistant Managers

761   Jimmy Wheeler.

762   Ian Branfoot.

763   Colin Lee.

764   Martin Allen.

765   Eddie Niedzwiecki.

766   Deepdale, home of Preston North End, before Reading's match there in February 2000.

767   Nigel Gibbs.

768   Dean Austin.

769   Pat "Packie" Bonner, who joined in 1998 as assistant to Tommy Burns.

770   John Gorman.

Quiz 78 – Reading & Middlesbrough

771   Ian Harte and Shane Long.

772   Leroy Lita.

773   Chris Riggott.

774   Paul Gascoigne. Paul Merson was also in the Boro team, but he wasn't substituted until the 85th minute, he was substituted after an hour.

775   Craig Hignett.

776   Nothing, He joined on a free transfer.

777   Dave Kitson, in the 55th minute. This was cancelled out by Tuncay in the 84th.

778   Chris Martin.

779   Seol Ki-Hyeon.

780   All 14 of them. None had previously played in the Premier League.

Quiz 79 – 1995/96 season

781   QPR.

782   Michael Meaker, bought for £550,000.

783   Simon Sheppard.

784   Paul Parker.

785   They had been 2-0 down when the match was abandoned after just 28 minutes. They also benefitted from an own goal in the replayed game.

786   Trevor Morley.

787   Leeds United. Reading lost 2-1 at Elland Road

788   Darren Caskey, signed from Tottenham for £700,000 and Nick Hammond, who arrived from Plymouth for £40,000.

789   3-0 to Reading, with goals scored by Martin Williams and two from Jimmy Quinn.

790   Seven. They were permanent signings Simon Sheppard, Boris Mihaylov, Nick Hammond plus loanees Chris Woods, Eric Nixon and Stephen Sutton - and also Jimmy Quinn who played as emergency 'keeper in a league match at home to West Brom.

Quiz 80 – World Cup Royals

791   Bulgaria.

792   Bobby Convey. He also came on as a substitute in the third group match.

793   Marcus Hahnemann.

794   The third-place play-off defeat to Italy.

795   Jón Daði Böðvarsson. He started in Iceland's second group match, against Nigeria.

796   Seol Ki-Hyeon, playing for South Korea, who won the match 2-1 after extra time.

797   Chris Gunter, for Wales.

798   *Chris Woods.*

799   *Gylfi Sigurðsson. He scored from the penalty spot against Croatia in World Cup 2018, but Iceland failed to qualify from the group stage.*

800   *Ray Houghton. He scored in this match, his 73rd cap, but Ireland lost 3-2.*

Quiz 81 – Reading & Millwall

801   *Shaun Cummings.*

802   *George Evans and Sam Smith.*

803   *Eamon Dunphy.*

804   *Bobby Convey.*

805   *Mathieu Manset.*

806   *Darius Henderson, in the 50th minute.*

807   *John Alexander.*

808   *Jón Daði Böðvarsson*

809   *Seven. He also booked two Millwall players.*

810   *Jake Cooper.*

Quiz 82 – 1996/97 season

811   *Wolves, managed by Mark McGhee, for a fee of £750,000. He was replaced by Barry Hunter, who joined for £400,000.*

812   *Sheffield United, at home in the league. He was sent off in the 81st minute of the game, but two minutes later Jimmy Quinn scored the only goal of the game to ensure victory.*

813   *Borislav Mihailov.*

814   *Crystal Palace. Trevor Morley scored Reading's only goal.*

815   *Graeme Souness.*

816   *Bolton, who had only survived a single season in the Premier League.*

817   *Trevor Morley.*

818   *The 96th.*

819   *Michael Gilkes - he'd signed for Wolves in March 1997 for £50,000.*

820   *Stuart Lovell. Due to this, he didn't start a match for Reading until December 1997.*

Quiz 83 – Managers (2)

821   *Celtic Park, Glasgow.*

822   *Alan Pardew and Brian McDermott.*

823   Ian Branfoot.

824   Roy Bentley.

825   Liverpool.

826   Fulham.

827   Johnny Cochrane.

828   Brendan Rodgers.

829   Jack Smith.

830   Scunthorpe Utd.

Quiz 84 – Reading & Newcastle

831   James Harper, in a 3-2 defeat.

832   Trevor Senior, although it was widely reported at the time to be Mick Tait.

833   Mark McGhee.

834   Danny Guthrie, prior to the away game at The Stadium of Light in December 2012.

835   Paul Brayson, who signed for a fee of £100,000.

836   Jimmy Crawford, signed for £50,000. He scored one goal in 24 appearances.

837   Dave Kitson, after 51 minutes.

838   Michael Owen. He did score against Reading the following season, though.

839   Michael Duberry.

840   Adam Le Fondre.

Quiz 85 – 1997/98 season

841   Tommy Burns.

842   Barnet.

843   Lee Hodges and Linvoy Primus, each for £250,000.

844   Oxford United, who they beat 2-1 through goals from Carl Asaba and Lee Hodges.

845   Phil Parkinson.

846   Nick Colgan, who joined on loan from Chelsea in February 1998.

847   The 3-0 defeat to Oxford at The Manor Ground on 17th March 1998.

848   Seven.

849   Six - home wins over Manchester City and Stoke, the two teams relegated with them.

850 38, their highest up to that point. Tommy Burns used 46 players the following season.

Quiz 86 – Ups and Downs

851 Seventeen - nine promotions and eight relegations.

852 Six times - 1926, 1979, 1986, 1994, 2006 and 2012.

853 28 points, in the 2012/13 Premier League season. That came from a 38-match season.

854 Five times. Four times in Division 3 (South) where only one team was promoted (1932, 1935, 1949 & 1952), plus 1995 where second place led to a play-off place due to league restructuring.

855 They were 25 points ahead of Watford, who were later promoted through the play-offs.

856 Just once, in 1998.

857 1970/71. Reading had a goal average of 0.565 compared to Walsall's 0.895.

858 The third tier, originally Division Three, where they've spent 30 seasons. They've spent eight seasons in tier 4, 21 in the second tier and three in the Premier League.

859 1983, when they finished fourth from bottom of Division Three.

860 16th in Division Four, in 1971/72.

Quiz 87 – Reading & Non-League Teams

861 Dunstable Town.

862 Vinnie Jones.

863 York City.

864 Barrow AFC.

865 Wokingham Town.

866 Rushden and Diamonds.

867 Plainmoor, home of Torquay United.

868 Grzegorz Rasiak.

869 Darlington. Reading won 4-2 on penalties.

870 Scarborough.

Quiz 88 – 1998/99 season

871 Gordon Neate.

872 Grant Brebner.

873 Mass Sarr, signed from Hajduk Split for £158,000.

874　The "Death Row Five" - Jason Bowen, Gareth Davies, James Lambert, Andy Legg and Steve Swales.

875　Peter van der Kwaak.

876　Jamie Cureton - playing for Bristol Rovers, for whom he scored four goals as his team won 6-0. The half time score was 0-0!

877　Danny Tiatto.

878　Manchester City. Reading lost 3-1.

879　Andy McLaren.

880　Graeme Murty.

Quiz 89 – Referees

881　Graham Poll.

882　Because of reports of homophobic chants from home supporters. An investigation later found no evidence of such chants.

883　Geoff Eltringham.

884　Stuart Attwell.

885　Geoff Eltringham.

886　1998, in the quarter-final tie in January at Elm Park.

887　Kingsley Royal - because clearly a seven-foot tall cuddly lion is easily mistaken for a footballer!

888　Mark Halsey.

889　Grant Hegley.

890　Keith Stroud.

Quiz 90 – Reading & Norwich City

891　Yann Kermorgant.

892　Robert Fleck.

893　Craig Bellamy.

894　Jake Cooper.

895　Peter Grant. He later became manager at Norwich.

896　4-4.

897　Shane Long. Both games were 2-0 wins for Reading.

898　Sheffield Wednesday. The player was Chris Woods.

899　Andy Hughes.

900　Andy Rinomhota.

Quiz 91 – 1999/2000 season

901   Byron Glasgow. He was sacked from the club, although they did pay the costs of a rehabilitation programme for him.

902   Gerard Lavin. As well as receiving a straight red card, he was later found guilty of assault and paid compensation to the supporter.

903   The 1-1 League Cup 2nd Round first leg draw at Bradford on 14th September 1999, although his fate was probably decided three days earlier as Reading lost 3-1 away at Bournemouth, including scoring two own goals.

904   "Players Are Not Trying Sufficiently."

905   Richard Carpenter. Casper later sued Carpenter and won undisclosed damages in an out-of-court settlement.

906   Away at Gillingham, in a 2-2 draw on January 3rd 2000.

907   Mark Nicholls. His loan move from Chelsea to Reading on 30th December 1999 was also the last transfer of the 20th century.

908   Portsmouth, for £150,000.

909   Ady Williams.

910   Darren Caskey.

Quiz 92 – Alan Pardew

911   The 2-0 home defeat to Huddersfield in March 1998, as caretaker manager following the dismissal of Terry Bullivant.

912   Crystal Palace.

913   Goalkeeper Phil Whitehead, signed from West Brom for £250,000.

914   Glenn Roeder.

915   Steve Coppell.

916   Terry Bullivant, appointed manager at the start of the 1997/98 season.

917   Kevin Dillon, who was shortly afterwards replaced Brian McDermott and Nick Hammond.

918   West Ham at the Boleyn Ground. The home team won 1-0, through an 18th minute Christian Dailly goal.

919   Barnet. His last match was a 4-0 defeat away to Hartlepool in April 1997.

920   3-0 to Reading, with two goals from Shaun Goater and one from Andy Hughes.

Quiz 93 – Reading & Nottingham

921   Ron Blackman.

922   James Lambert.

923   Steve Stone.

924   Darren Caskey departed, whilst Andy Hughes came in the opposite direction.

925   Simon Church. The other goals were scored by Ian Harte, Jem Karacan and Jimmy Kebe.

926   Jamie Cureton in the 14th and 44th minutes. Ex-Magpie Andy Hughes had opened the scoring after four minutes, and Alex Smith scored in the 45th.

927   Football League Division One. Notts County had been founder members of the Football League in 1888.

928   Trent Bridge Cricket Ground.

929   Simon Cox.

930   Garath McCleary in the 10th minute and Chris Gunter after 62.

Quiz 94 – 2000/01 season

931   Nicky Forster.

932   Jamie Cureton, purchased from Bristol Rovers.

933   Maurice Evans. He is commemorated by a blue plaque at the stadium with the words: "Player, Manager, Gentleman."

934   "What a waste of petrol" - this was at the height of the fuel crisis of that year.

935   Eighteen - of those, Jamie Cureton scored six goals and Martin Butler five, with a hat-trick each, as Reading scored five in a match twice and four goals once.

936   Oxford United - with goals from Tony Rougier in the 79th and 88th minute, after Darren Caskey and Jamie Cureton had previously scored.

937   Millwall, who won the match 4-3 despite goals from Sammy Igoe, Darren Caskey and Jamie Cureton.

938   Graeme Murty.

939   At Layer Road against Colchester United. They took the lead through Jamie Cureton but lost to a 44th minute penalty.

940   100 - 86 in the league, seven in the FA Cup, one in the League Cup, two in the Associate Member's Cup plus four the play-offs. 58 of these were scored by Jamie Cureton and Martin Butler.

Quiz 95 – Scottish Royals

941 *Stuart Lovell.*
942 *Five. Irishman Jimmy Crawford and Englishman Paul Brayson were the only exceptions.*
943 *Jim McIntyre.*
944 *Andy McLaren.*
945 *Grant Brebner.*
946 *Manchester United.*
947 *Aberdeen.*
948 *Graeme Murty.*
949 *Tom McIntyre.*
950 *Stuart Gray, son of Eddie Gray of Leeds United.*

Quiz 96 – Reading & Portsmouth

951 *Kevin Dillon.*
952 *Fulham. The Portsmouth defence allowed 5' 9" tall Danny Murphy to out-jump them to score the game's only goal from a corner.*
953 *Linvoy Primus.*
954 *Most goals in a single match - Reading lost 7-4, and also (jointly) the most different scorers in a Premier League match, with nine scorers.*
955 *Benjani.*
956 *Shaka Hislop.*
957 *Jamie Ashdown.*
958 *Ibrahima Sonko.*
959 *Matt Robinson and Sammy Igoe.*
960 *Glen Little.*

Quiz 97 – 2001/02 Season

961 *Spurs.*
962 *"Reading Fans Everywhere."*
963 *Charlton.*
964 *Darius Henderson.*
965 *None.*
966 *York City.*
967 *The County Ground, Swindon. The match ended 0-0 but there was no love shown that night in a match with three red cards.*
968 *Just the one, a 2-0 win at Chesterfield. They drew the other nine matches.*

969   *The 77th minute.*

970   *Five players - Ivar Ingimarsson, Michael Dobson, Steve Sidwell, Stephen Hunt and Lloyd Owusu. They also later acquired Brentford's manager and assistant manager, Steve Coppell and Wally Downes.*

Quiz 98 – Own Goals

971   *Darlington, who won 2-0.*

972   *Bolton Wanderers. Two late goals from Kevin Doyle and a third from Stephen Hunt secured the victory.*

973   *Terry Bell.*

974   *Jason Kavanagh.*

975   *Tony Rougier.*

976   *Graeme Murty - the second ricochet off a Reading defender.*

977   *Tobias Figueiredo.*

978   *Ivar Ingimarsson.*

979   *Neill Collins.*

980   *Ady Williams.*

Quiz 99 – Reading & Queens Park Rangers

981   *Alex McCarthy.*

982   *John Swift.*

983   *Jamie Cureton.*

984   *"Jacks" - called to him by Steve Sidwell. This is footballers' shorthand for "leave it."*

985   *Graeme Murty, from the penalty spot.*

986   *They "Raised the Hoops", blue and white hoops running all around the stadium. Even some QPR fans joined in!*

987   *Mikele Leigertwood.*

988   *Pavel Pogrebnyak.*

989   *Tiago Ilori, sent off in the 2-0 away defeat in August, and Yann Kermorgant, red-carded in Reading's 1-0 home win.*

990   *1926, in September.*

Quiz 100 – 2002/03 Season

991   *Marcus Hahnemann, who signed from Fulham.*

992   *The bankruptcy of ITV Digital and the loss of expected TV money from them.*

993 Matt Upson, who joined from Arsenal. He played 14 league matches, of which Reading won nine, with only five goals conceded from these 14 matches.

994 John Mackie and Carl Asaba, who was then with Sheffield United.

995 Steve Sidwell, who signed from Arsenal having previously been on loan at Brighton and Brentford. He scored twice in the team's 5-2 win away at Burnley.

996 Walsall.

997 Colchester United.

998 Preston, who also had two players sent off.

999 Peter Castle.

1000 Nicky Forster.

Quiz 101 – Quiz Reading & Sheffield United

1001 James Harper.

1002 Paddy Kenny.

1003 Brynjar Gunnarsson.

1004 Chris Armstrong.

1005 Billy Sharp.

1006 Ulises de la Cruz.

1007 Ibrahima Sonko.

1008 Darius Henderson.

1009 Nick Blackman.

1010 Brian Howard.

Quiz 102 – Reading & Sheffield Wednesday

1011 Kevin Doyle.

1012 Lloyd Owusu.

1013 3-1 to Wednesday, with two goals from Atdhe Nuhiu and one from George Boyd. Reading's consolation was a Cameron Dawson own goal.

1014 Keiren Westwood in the match at the Madejski in August 2019, and Osaze Urhoghide in the return at Hillsborough.

1015 Jimmy Kebe and Grzegorz Rasiak.

1016 Khalifa Cisse.

1017 Michail Antonio.

1018 1-0 to Reading, with the only goal scored by Bill Johnstone.

1019 Jamie Cureton.

1020 Lucas João.

Quiz 103 – 2003/04 Season

1021 *Five - Nicky Shorey after 78 minutes in this match, Adrian Viveash in March 2003, Andy Legg and Andy Bernal in March 1998 and Bobby Mihaylov in August 1996.*

1022 *It was against Wimbledon, who were playing at Selhurst Park after leaving Plough Lane. Home fans boycotted the match due to the team's aim to relocate to Milton Keynes.*

1023 *Bas Savage.*

1024 *Glen Little and Luke Chadwick, who scored Burnley's third goal.*

1025 *Wimbledon.*

1026 *Jobi McAnuff.*

1027 *Preston. Reading's other goal in the first match was scored by Shaun Goater in the 8th minute.*

1028 *Dave Kitson. Although signed from Cambridge on 26th December, he was carrying a slight injury at that time.*

1029 *Ivar Ingimarsson after 39 minutes, Dave Kitson after 45, and Dean Morgan after 90 minutes.*

1030 *Vicarage Road, Watford, for whom Ashley Young scored the only goal.*

Quiz 104 – Steve Coppell

1031 *Tranmere Rovers, for whom he made 38 appearances between 1973 and 1975.*

1032 *Economic History.*

1033 *Southampton, who won 1-0 in 1976.*

1034 *Most consecutive appearances for an outfield player, with 207 from 1977 to 1981.*

1035 *33 days, and 6 games - the shortest managerial reign in their history.*

1036 *The 2-1 victory over Gillingham at the Madejski Stadium on 14th October 2003.*

1037 *LMA League Manager of the Year. It was the second season running he had won this award.*

1038 *In Coppell's car parking space at the Madejski Stadium.*

1039 *Jay Tabb.*

1040 *Kerala Blasters.*

Quiz 105 – 2004/05 season

1041 *Paul Brooker.*

1042 *15. Brighton's Maheta Molango scored this early goal, but Reading won this home match 3-2 through goals from Dave Kitson, James Harper and Nicky Forster.*

1043 *Bobby Convey.*

1044 *Sunderland. Reading won 1-0 at home in August 2004 and 2-1 at The Stadium of Light in April 2005.*

1045 *By helicopter - he had a helicopter pilot's licence and his own chopper, which cost him £2M.*

1046 *Coventry City.*

1047 *Watford, through goals from Ibrahima Sonko after three minutes, Steve Sidwell after 76 and Lloyd Owusu after 88.*

1048 *11 matches, seven of which were draws. They also had one defeat, one draw and one win (after extra time) in the FA Cup in this 11 week period.*

1049 *Dave Kitson, in a 3-1 home win over Alan Pardew's West Ham.*

1050 *The JJB Stadium, Wigan. Reading lost 3-1, again failing to take advantage of an outside chance of promotion.*

Quiz 106 – The 106 Team

1051 *One. Chris Makin had played for Oldham and Sunderland at that level.*

1052 *Leroy Lita, purchased from Bristol City for £1M in the summer of 2005.*

1053 *John Halls, who scored in the 3-1 home defeat of Stoke in April 2006.*

1054 *Three - James Harper, Steve Sidwell and Graham Stack.*

1055 *Eight: Kevin Doyle, Shane Long, Stephen Hunt, Leroy Lita, Brynjar Gunnarsson, John Oster, Chris Makin and Eric Chukwunyelu Obinna.*

1056 *95. There were also four own goals scored by opposition players, making the overall total 99 goals scored.*

1057 *Glen Little and John Oster.*

1058 *Stephen Hunt, who came off the bench 35 times.*

1059 *19 - and of these John Halls, Shane Long and Graham Stack started only one match each, and Stephen Hunt three matches.*

1060 *Chris Makin - the only such player to miss the defeats to Plymouth and Luton.*

Quiz 107 – Reading & Southampton

1061 *They used their share of the gate money to lodge a successful appeal with the FA over Southampton's use of two ineligible players, and were awarded the tie as Southampton were disqualified.*

1062 *Jason Roberts, after 19 minutes. Adam le Fondre scored in the 73rd and 91st minutes to secure victory.*

1063 *Rickie Lambert after 48 minutes.*

1064 *Joseph Mills.*

1065 *Johnny Walker.*

1066 *Shane Long, who scored against Watford after just 7.69 seconds in April 2019.*

1067 *Lee Nogan after 28 minutes and Trevor Morley after 64.*

1068 *Nigel Adkins, who had been appointed to the role just over a week earlier.*

1069 *Steve Richardson.*

1070 *He felt that the pitch was too icy to be played on. Mick Gooding and referee Graham Poll disagreed, and Reading won the tie 3-1.*

Quiz 108 – 2005/06 season

1071 *Chris Makin.*

1072 *Catalyst.*

1073 *Glen Little, who scored at Brighton and Preston in August 2005.*

1074 *Ibrahima Sonko, with an 88th minute header.*

1075 *Gresty Road, where they beat Crewe Alexandra.*

1076 *Watford.*

1077 *Shane Long - he scored once in the away match at Pride Park in December 2005 and twice in the home match on 1st April which secured the Championship title.*

1078 *His bench jacket - after first asking Ron Grant, the kitman, if that was OK!*

1079 *Four - Millwall, Brighton, Derby and Cardiff (twice, home and away).*

1080 *They are the only team ever to win promotion to the Premier League during Greenwich Mean Time - the clocks didn't go forward into BST until the next day.*

Quiz 109 – Behind the scenes

1081 *Alan Pardew.*

1082 *Boyd Butler.*

1083 Annie Bassett.

1084 Supporters' Trust At Reading.

1085 Ron Grant.

1086 Gordon Neate, who had been with the club as player and groundsman for over 53 years.

1087 Brian Tevreden.

1088 Mike Lewis.

1089 Jon Fearn.

1090 Nick Hammond.

Quiz 110 – Reading & The Southwest

1091 Andy Gurney.

1092 Yakou Mëïté. Josh Barrett scored Reading's two earlier goals.

1093 Danny Bailey.

1094 The ten goals were scored by just five players, all of whom scored two goals each.

1095 Ibrahima Sonko.

1096 Yeovil had three players sent off in the second-half. Reading were still unable to beat them, though, and needed an own goal to secure a point.

1097 Andy Rogers.

1098 Jake Taylor.

1099 Nick Chadwick.

1100 The perimeter wall in front of them collapsed.

Quiz 111 – 2006/07 season

1101 Dave Kitson, in the 3-2 win over Middlesbrough at the MadStad.

1102 Seol Ki-Hyeon.

1103 Manchester United - twice in the league, and in a FA Cup 5th Round replay at the Madejski after drawing 1-1 at Old Trafford.

1104 Peter Máté.

1105 Three, all in the Premier League. They were Ibrahima Sonko at Aston Villa, Andre Bikey at home to Chelsea and Sam Sodje at Manchester Utd.

1106 Oliver Holt.

1107 Kevin Doyle, after 36 and 78 minutes.

1108 Greg Halford.

1109 Kevin Doyle, with an 85th minute penalty and a goal after 89 minutes. Stephen Hunt added a third in injury time.

1110 *Five: Manchester City, Sheffield United, West Ham, Fulham and Bolton.*

Quiz 112 – Royal Flops

1111 *Simon Sheppard.*

1112 *Sean Evers.*

1113 *Peter van der Kwaak.*

1114 *Daniel Carriço, signed from Sporting CP in January 2013 for £675,000.*

1115 *Sixteen. Reading scored just one goal in reply.*

1116 *Royston Drenthe.*

1117 *Emerse Fae.*

1118 *Zat Knight.*

1119 *Mass Sarr.*

1120 *Paul Brayson.*

Quiz 113 – Reading & Stoke City

1121 *Jamie Cureton. He'd previously scored four goals in a game for Bristol Rovers at the Madejski.*

1122 *Leroy Lita.*

1123 *James Henry.*

1124 *Kyle Lightbourne.*

1125 *John Halls. This match was his only league start for Reading.*

1126 *Modou Barrow, in the 4th minute of added time. .*

1127 *Andy Griffin.*

1128 *Dave Kitson and Ibrahima Sonko.*

1129 *Mark McKeever.*

1130 *Michael Duberry.*

Quiz 114 – 2007/08 season

1131 *Everton, who they beat 1-0 in their first home match of the season, through a 45th minute Stephen Hunt goal.*

1132 *Bolton Wanderers, at the Reebok Stadium.*

1133 *Stephen Hunt's.*

1134 *Brynjar Gunnarsson.*

1135 *Jermain Defoe.*

1136 *Lens.*

1137 Andre Bikey, with goals after 31 and 79 minutes.

1138 33 matches.

1139 Brazil, in a friendly international which ended 1-1.

1140 James Harper.

Quiz 115 - Elm Park (2)

1141 1954.

1142 Network SouthEast.

1143 Fleetwood Mac – although torrential rain meant the event was abandoned with 5,000 people in the ground.

1144 1984.

1145 The "Spalding Avenue" - so called because it was financed by prospective Liberal candidate for the town, Mr Spalding.

1146 Michael Meaker, in the 2-0 defeat of Stoke on 4th April 1998.

1147 6,000. It was increased to 12,500 later in the season.

1148 He treated the pitch with undiluted weedkiller which killed most of the grass.

1149 The 1-0 FA Cup win over Birmingham City in November 1992.

1150 New Zealand.

Quiz 116 – Reading & Sunderland

1151 Dave Kitson, with goals in the 77th minute and an 83rd minute penalty.

1152 Greg Halford. They also made a slight profit on the deal.

1153 Vito Mannone.

1154 2012. It was postponed at 1.45pm after local torrential rain - but many suspected there was a problem with the pitch which had been newly re-laid after a series of pop concerts that summer.

1155 John Oster.

1156 Stephen Hunt.

1157 Liam Kelly.

1158 Jimmy Kebe.

1159 Charlie Hurley and Ian Porterfield.

1160 John O'Shea, who was sent off in a 3-0 win over Hull at the Madejski for a foul on Chris Martin.

Quiz 117 – 2008/09 season

1161 Dagenham & Redbridge.

1162 Noel Hunt, who'd signed from Dundee for £600,000.

1163 Kevin Doyle, against Crystal Palace in August and Sheffield Wednesday 18 days later.

1164 Wolves, who they beat 3-0.

1165 Brian Jensen.

1166 Neil Collins.

1167 Jon Stead, in Ipswich's 2-0 home victory in September 2008 and their 1-0 away win in March 2009.

1168 Sheffield United.

1169 Blackpool - with first-half goals from Jem Karacan and Noel Hunt.

1170 Marek Matejovsky.

Quiz 118 – The Irish Connection

1171 Pat Dolan, Eamonn's twin brother, who recommended these players to Eamonn.

1172 Jimmy Crawford.

1173 Hurling.

1174 Joe Gamble.

1175 Jimmy Quinn.

1176 John O'Shea, with 118 caps, behind Shay Given (134) and Robbie Keane (146).

1177 Dave Bacuzzi.

1178 Noel Hunt.

1179 Paul McShane.

1180 Eamon Dunphy.

Quiz 119 – Reading & Swansea City

1181 Martin Butler, with goals after 53, 57 and 88 minutes.

1182 Modou Barrow.

1183 Liam Rosenior.

1184 Kevin Doyle, after 26 and 90 minutes.

1185 Scott Sinclair.

1186 That victory in the 1926/27 FA Cup quarter-final marked the only time Reading had reached the semi-finals of that competition - a feat they repeated in 2015.

1187 Callum Harriott, after 77 minutes.

1188 Nicky Forster.

1189 Michel Vorm.

1190 Alex McCarthy.

Quiz 120 – 2009/10 season

1191 Gylfi Sigurðsson, with a goal scored from 35 yards.

1192 Doncaster Rovers.

1193 Away at Barnsley at the end of August 2009. Alex Pearce scored after 29 minutes and Noel Hunt after 53 and 54 minutes.

1194 £6.5M.

1195 Scunthorpe United. Grzegorz Rasiak scored Reading's goal after 16 minutes.

1196 Jimmy Kebe.

1197 Shane Long.

1198 Five, scoring twice against Bristol City and once against QPR, Leicester and West Brom.

1199 Peterborough.

1200 Derby County, at the Madejski in March Bertrand scored the third goal in Reading's 4-1 win.

Quiz 121 – Brian McDermott

1201 Nick Hammond.

1202 Chief Scout, replacing Maurice Evans in this role.

1203 Arsenal, who he joined in 1977 and left in 1984.

1204 Simon Church, in the 1-1 draw at Bristol City on 19th December 2009.

1205 Eamonn Dolan.

1206 Slough Town - "he used to manage Slough".

1207 Neil Warnock.

1208 Massimo Cellino.

1209 Blackburn Rovers. Reading beat them 1-0 at the Madejski in December 2015, but lost 3-1 at Ewood Park in the last match of the season.

1210 Liverpool, beaten 2-1 after extra time in an FA Cup 3rd Round replay at Anfield.

Quiz 122 – Reading & The Rest (1)

1211 Nicky Shorey.

1212 Liam Kelly, after 71 and 86 minutes.

1213 Sam Baldock and Danny Loader.

1214 Jamie Cureton.

1215 *Hope Akpan.*

1216 *Matej Vydra.*

1217 *Colchester United.*

1218 *Michael Gilkes.*

1219 *The Pirelli Stadium, where they beat Burton Albion 4-2.*

1220 *75.*

Quiz 123 – 2010/11 season

1221 *Scunthorpe United. Gylfi Sigurðsson scored their goal after 26 minutes.*

1222 *Ian Harte.*

1223 *1899 Hoffenheim in the German Bundesliga.*

1224 *Grant Holt, for a tackle on Ian Harte. At that point Reading were 3-1 down.*

1225 *Middlesbrough.*

1226 *Mathieu Manset, who signed from Hereford United in Jan. 2011.*

1227 *Eight - there was also a 1-0 defeat in the FA Cup to Manchester City in the middle of the winning run.*

1228 *Sheffield United, who beat Reading 3-2.*

1229 *Coventry City, in April 2011.*

1230 *Jobi McAnuff, who made the score 3-0 to Reading.*

Quiz 124 – League Cup (2)

1231 *Peterborough United.*

1232 *Wolves.*

1233 *Nick Blackman.*

1234 *0-0 after extra time. Reading won 6-5 on penalties.*

1235 *Jimmy Quinn.*

1236 *Ady Williams.*

1237 *Phil Parkinson.*

1238 *Arsenal, who beat them 3-0 at Highbury.*

1239 *David Mooney & Nicholas Bignall.*

1240 *The Milk Marketing Board - it was known as "The Milk Cup".*

Quiz 125 – Reading & The Rest (2)

1241 *Matt Mills.*

1242 *Yaya Sanogo scored three for Charlton, and Deniss Rakels got the last-minute winner.*

1243 Stevenage.

1244 Martin Butler.

1245 Neil Lennon.

1246 Moss Rose, home of Macclesfield Town.

1247 Rotherham United.

1248 Steve Hetzke.

1249 Carl Asaba.

1250 Morecambe and Fleetwood.

Quiz 126 – 2011/12 season

1251 Kaspars Gorkss.

1252 Three. Ian Harte and Noel Hunt missed the first two before Hal Robson-Kanu scored the third as Reading lost 2-1.

1253 The Keepmoat Stadium, Doncaster Rovers. Although a modern stadium it was not fitted with undersoil heating.

1254 Away to West Ham in March 2012.

1255 Hull City, on 21st January 2012. Reading lost 1-0 to a Robbie Brady goal.

1256 17 out of 23, with two draws and only four defeats. This included a run of 15 wins in 17 matches between late January and mid-April

1257 Crystal Palace, with a 2-2 draw - although they didn't know that until later that evening when Southampton lost away at Middlesbrough.

1258 Jason Roberts.

1259 Birmingham City, 2-0.

1260 Garath McCleary, who joined from Nottingham Forest in 2012.

Quiz 127 – Play-offs (3)

1261 Away to Wolves in 2003, 27,678.

1262 Stephen Dobbie. He played in the 2010 and 2012 play-off finals with Blackpool, failing to win promotion only in 2012.

1263 Kevin Nicholls.

1264 Barcelona and Manchester Utd, in the Champions League Final.

1265 Graham Alexander.

1266 Stuart Lovell. Lee Nogan scored the other in a 3-1 win.

1267 Jem Karacan.

1268 Alex Rae, as Wolves won 1-0.

1269 Fulham's Kevin McDonald.

1270 *Four - Nathan Tyson v Wolves, Andre Bikey v Burnley, Jay Tabb (as a sub) v Swansea, Paul McShane v Fulham.*

Quiz 128 – Reading & Tottenham

1271 *Johnny Brooks.*

1272 *Robbie Keane, in the 16th minute of his team's 1-0 win.*

1273 *7-1 to Tottenham.*

1274 *Darren Caskey.*

1275 *3-1 to Spurs.*

1276 *Nicky Shorey.*

1277 *Dimitar Berbatov.*

1278 *Stephen Hunt.*

1279 *Tom Huddlestone.*

1280 *Dave Kitson, who scored twice in five minutes in Reading's 6-4 defeat.*

Quiz 129 – 2012/13 season

1281 *Pavel Pogrebnyak. He was rumoured to have been signed by Anton Zingarevich on wages of £65,000 a week.*

1282 *Danny Guthrie.*

1283 *16 - Premier League wins of 5-2 away and 4-1 at home, plus the infamous 7-5 League Cup win at The Madejski in October*

1284 *Adam Federici.*

1285 *Everton, with a 2-1 home win on 17th November*

1286 *Away at Newcastle to secure a 2-1 win, and 11 days later against Chelsea at the MadStad to earn a 2-2 draw.*

1287 *Away at Old Trafford in the Premier League in March 2013. Reading lost 1-0, to a Wayne Rooney goal.*

1288 *The Emirates Stadium, where they lost 4-1 to Arsenal.*

1289 *Fulham, who they beat 4-2 at Craven Cottage in May 2013.*

1290 *Jobi McAnuff.*

Quiz 130 – Transfer Fees

1291 *Shaka Hislop, who moved to Newcastle for £1.575M.*

1292 *Borislav Mihailov.*

1293 *Darren Caskey.*

1294 *£2.5M.*

1295 *Carl Asaba, who joined from Brentford.*

1296 *The initial £6.8M for the sale of Gylfi Sigurðsson beat the previous record of £6.5M received for Kevin Doyle, just over a year earlier.*

1297 *Bobby Convey, for £815,000.*

1298 *Ronnie Dix.*

1299 *Internazionale, for an estimated final figure of £8M.*

1300 *Colchester United.*

Quiz 131 – Reading & Watford

1301 *John Eustace.*

1302 *Adrian Mariappa.*

1303 *Jem Karacan, in the 41st and 70th minutes.*

1304 *Nigel Gibbs.*

1305 *Kaspars Gorkss.*

1306 *2002/03. He came off the bench in the 80th minute of a 3-0 win to Reading.*

1307 *Lee Nogan.*

1308 *0-0 in both matches.*

1309 *Roger Joslyn.*

1310 *They finished with 81 points - 25 behind Reading's total.*

Quiz 132 – 2013/14 season

1311 *1899 Hoffenheim.*

1312 *Jay Tabb. He'd never scored for Reading in 104 appearances!*

1313 *Jordan Obita.*

1314 *Michail Antonio, after 25 minutes.*

1315 *Bolton Wanderers.*

1316 *Kevin Doyle.*

1317 *Manchester City Under-21s.*

1318 *The urgent need to pay a £1.6M tax bill!*

1319 *Anton Zingarevich, Chris Samuelson and Andrew Obolensky.*

1320 *Brighton, who won 2-1 at Nottingham Forest.*

Quiz 133 – Welsh Royals

1321 *Chris Gunter.*

1322 *Wrexham.*

1323 *Mark Bowen.*

1324 *Seven: home and away against both Cardiff and Swansea in the Championship, two play-off semi-finals against Cardiff, and the play-off final against Swansea.*

1325 *Andy Legg.*

1326 *Hal Robson-Kanu, nominated for his Cruyff turn and goal in Wales' Euro 2016 3–1 quarter-final win over Belgium in Lille.*

1327 *Lee Nogan and Ady Williams.*

1328 *Jeff Hopkins.*

1329 *Jason Bowen, Gareth Davies and Andy Legg.*

1330 *Their 2-0 win at Somerton Park in October 1985 saw them set the record for most successive league wins at the start of a season.*

Quiz 134 – Reading & West Brom

1331 *Leroy Lita, with goals in the 51st, 66th and 93rd minutes. Reading had been 2-0 down.*

1332 *Richard Chaplow.*

1333 *Shane Long.*

1334 *Jonathan Bond.*

1335 *Romelu Lukaku, after 16 and 69 minutes. Reading scored three times in the last ten minutes to grab a 3-2 win.*

1336 *Paul McShane.*

1337 *He was hit by a coin thrown by one of his own team's supporters.*

1338 *Gylfi Sigurðsson.*

1339 *Nicky Shorey.*

1340 *Vikings.*

Quiz 135 – 2014/15 season

1341 *Andrija Novakovich.*

1342 *Glenn Murray, who scored twice in Reading's 3-0 home win over Fulham in September 2014.*

1343 *Wolves. Jake Taylor and Glenn Murray scored Reading's other two goals.*

1344 *The 6-1 loss to Birmingham City at St. Andrews in December 2014.*

1345 *Norwich City.*

1346 *Yakubu, away at Derby.*

1347 *Chelsea.*

1348 *They had broken financial regulations by taking out loans of £10.5M and £5.6M from Vibrac Corporation.*

1349 *Somersaults! Reading were censured by the FA for this - and also the ill-advised music played to accompany him.*

1350 *Adam Federici saved a penalty taken by Darren Bent.*

Quiz 136 – Loan Players

1351 *Ovie Ejaria.*

1352 *Dave Kitson - he scored twice in 12 games as Reading lost in the play-offs to Burnley.*

1353 *Sekou Baradji, who played in the 2-1 home win over Sheffield United, as well as two League Cup matches.*

1354 *Dundee United.*

1355 *Billy Sharp, who was on loan from Southampton.*

1356 *Chelsea.*

1357 *Blackburn Rovers.*

1358 *Hartlepool United.*

1359 *Sheffield Wednesday.*

1360 *Alex McCarthy.*

Quiz 137 – Reading & West Ham

1361 *Steve Mautone.*

1362 *Anton Ferdinand.*

1363 *None. Their only cup meeting to date is the League Cup tie at the Madejski in September 2001, which Reading won on penalties after it ended goalless.*

1364 *Reading 6 (SIX), West Ham Nil.*

1365 *Alan Curbishley. Alan Pardew had been sacked by West Ham just 21 days earlier.*

1366 *Trevor Morley.*

1367 *Seol Ki-Hyeon.*

1368 *Kevin Nolan.*

1369 *West Ham 2, Reading 4, with goals from Kaspars Gorkss, Noel Hunt, Ian Harte (pen) and Mikele Leigertwood.*

1370 *He adjusted his socks!*

Quiz 138 – 2015/16 season

1371 *Paul McShane.*

1372 *Michael Hector.*

1373 *Ipswich Town.*

1374 He had spoken with Fulham about their managerial vacancy - but had also decided not to accept that role. However, it may have something to do with only having won 13 out of 44 league matches!

1375 Under-21s manager Martin Kuhl.

1376 A 1-0 home Championship win over Blackburn in December 2015, with Danny Williams scoring the only goal.

1377 George Evans from Manchester City and Yann Kermorgant from Bournemouth.

1378 Matej Vydra.

1379 Jake Cooper. At that point the score was 0-0, but Reading lost 2-0.

1380 Nick Blackman.

Quiz 139 – FA Cup (2)

1381 Molineux, Wolverhampton.

1382 Cheltenham Town.

1383 Hal Robson-Kanu, Garath McCleary and Jamie Mackie.

1384 Scott Taylor.

1385 Yakubu.

1386 Corinthians.

1387 Simon Cox.

1388 Barnsley.

1389 Alexis Sanchez.

1390 Six times. In 1900/01, 2009/10, 2010/11 & 2015/16 they were knocked out at this stage, and in 1926/27 & 2014/15 they went on to the semi-finals.

Quiz 140 – Reading & Wigan Athletic

1391 August 1978 at Elm Park, in a 2-0 home win. This was only Wigan Athletic's third Football League match after replacing Southport.

1392 Emile Heskey, in a 1-0 home win and a 3-2 away defeat for Wigan.

1393 Jason Roberts.

1394 George Puscas, with a five-minute hat-trick.

1395 Pavel Pogrebnyak.

1396 Six - a 1-1 draw in the league match at the JJB, a 1-0 win for Reading at home in the league, and a 2-1 play-off semi-final win for Reading after a 0-0 away first leg.

1397 Mark Bowen.

1398 0-0. At half time in that game, Fulham were losing to Manchester City and would have been all but relegated, but they scored three times in the second-half to win, and ultimately stayed up at Reading's expense.
1399 Andy McLaren.
1400 Ali Al Habsi.

Quiz 141 – 2016/17 season

1401 Sumrith Thanakarnjanasuth - more popularly known as "Tiger".
1402 Danzell Gravenberch.
1403 John Swift.
1404 Alex Oxlade-Chamberlain.
1405 Fulham.
1406 He scored his 249th goal for Man Utd - equalling Bobby Charlton's record.
1407 Dominic Samuel. He scored at home to Burton and away to Blackburn.
1408 Norwich City. The match ended 7-1 to the Canaries.
1409 Joseph Mendes.
1410 The Football League Trophy, which, controversially, featured Under-23 teams from Category One Academies.

Quiz 142 – Managers (3)

1411 Maurice Evans.
1412 Roy Bentley.
1413 Steve Clarke.
1414 Terry Bullivant.
1415 West Ham.
1416 Rio Ave Futebol Clube of Portugal.
1417 Mick Gooding, Jeff Hopkins, Jimmy Quinn & Ady Williams.
1418 Paul Clement. In comparison, Brendan Rodgers won six out of his 23 matches in charge.
1419 Charlie Hurley.
1420 Brian McDermott was replaced by Nigel Adkins.

Quiz 143 – Reading & Wimbledon

1421 Jamie Mackie.
1422 Lawrie Sanchez, who scored the only goal in the 1988 FA Cup Final.
1423 Tennai Watson.

1424 Shaun Goater.

1425 Jobi McAnuff and Mikele Leigertwood.

1426 Dave Beasant.

1427 Wally Downes.

1428 A 0-0 draw.

1429 Vinnie Jones.

1430 Reading Town.

Quiz 144 – 2017/18 season

1431 Tarique Fosu-Henry.

1432 Tiago Ilori, sent off after 56 minutes for a challenge on Pawel Wszolek.

1433 Jón Daði Böðvarsson in July and David Edwards six weeks later.

1434 They beat Nottingham Forest 3-1 at the Madejski on 31st October and
      Derby 4-2 at Pride Park four days later.

1435 Leandro Bacuna.

1436 Tommy Elphick.

1437 Burton Albion, who they beat 3-1 away on 30th January 2018. They
      lost ten and drew seven of the other league games in this period.

1438 Chris Gunter - only his second League goal in six seasons with the club
      at that time.

1439 A 4-0 win for Ipswich.

1440 Away at Cardiff City.

Quiz 145 – The Madejski Stadium (2)

1441 The Cook Islands.

1442 Elton John.

1443 Stuart Hall.

1444 Jamie Cureton, for Bristol Rovers against Reading in January 1999.

1445 Jamie Cureton, in Reading's 4-0 defeat of Brentford in September 2000.

1446 "AllStarz Summer Party".

1447 A staircase down the steep grass bank that came out by the roundabout
      on Shooters Way.

1448 Burnley, who drew 1-1 in the league. Their goal was scored by Andy
      Payton after 76 minutes.

1449 "Picnic on the Pitch" - the event was, sadly, plagued by rain!

1450 Maurice Evans and Roy Tranter.

Quiz 146 – Reading & Wolves

1451 Mick Gooding, signed for £65,000 in September 1989.

1452 Paul Bodin was sent off, after Gareth Davies had ruffled the hair of 17-year-old Robbie Keane, who fell to the ground clutching his face. Reading didn't appeal against the red card - presumably losing Bodin to suspension was less damaging than losing Davies!

1453 Dave Kitson after 29 minutes and Bobby Convey after 64.

1454 Wayne Hennessey.

1455 Andy Hughes.

1456 Ivar Ingimarsson. He was signed for just £100,000.

1457 Paul Brayson.

1458 Kevin Doyle and Marcus Hahnemann.

1459 Seol Ki-Hyeon, signed for £1.5M.

1460 Four. They drew the first, in March 1996 1-1, then won the next four with an aggregate score of 10-3.

Quiz 147 – 2018/19 season

1461 Bolton, who won through a goal from Yanic Wildschut.

1462 Marc McNulty.

1463 Away at Deepdale, Preston, where they won 3-2 with goals from Sam Baldock, Tiago Ilori and Leandro Bacuna.

1464 Hull City, achieved with goals from Sam Baldock, Jón Daði Böðvarsson and Andy Yiadom.

1465 Under-23s manager Scott Marshall.

1466 Gianluca Nani.

1467 Shrewsbury Town.

1468 Chelsea.

1469 "Technical Consultant".

1470 0-0 - against West Brom and Birmingham.

Quiz 148 – Transfer Trails (4)

1471 Neil Webb.

1472 Shaka Hislop.

1473 Adrian Mariappa.

1474 Mark McGhee.

1475 Chris Gunter.

1476 Wayne Bridge.

1477 Tyler Blackett.

1478 Steve Wood.

1479 Michael Gilkes.

1480 Kevin Doyle.

Quiz 149 – Reading & Yorkshire

1481 Barnsley.

1482 Sean Morrison.

1483 Matt Mills.

1484 Neil Webb.

1485 Filipe Morais.

1486 Steve Francis.

1487 Garath McCleary.

1488 Pavel Pogrebnyak, with 87th- and 95th-minute goals.

1489 Ivar Ingimarsson.

1490 Oliver Norwood, who joined from Huddersfield.

Quiz 150 – Royals Records

1491 Crystal Palace.

1492 1,103 minutes.

1493 Thirteen.

1494 Martin Hicks. These were made between 1978 and 1991.

1495 18–0, at Preston North End in the 1st Round of the FA Cup in January 1894.

1496 Ronnie Blackman, with 39 scored in 1951/52.

1497 Vicarage Road, Watford, in a 3-0 win in April 2003.

1498 Losers of the highest-scoring matches ever in that competition - 7-5 in the League Cup and 7-4 (and also 6-4) in the Premier League.

1499 33,042.

1500 191, scored in his two spells between 1983–1987 and 1988–1992.

By the Same Author – "*The Sum of the Parts*"

The three years after 2005 were a special time for Reading Football Club, a provincial team with a long but largely undistinguished history.

Suddenly, all the pieces of the football jigsaw clicked into place to create what was virtually a perfect team – a team that won the Football League Championship in great style, amassing a record-breaking total of 106 points in the process. The next season, their first ever in the Premier League, they confounded pundits and opponents alike by finishing eighth and narrowly missing out on European qualification.

For everyone associated with Reading Football Club, this was a time of wonder and excitement, a time when every match seemed to bring ever greater highs and exceed all previous expectations. But it was short-lived, and the following season they were relegated back to the Championship.

Just what happened in this brief period to transform a group of relatively unknown players into such a perfect team? Most were either at the start of their careers or coming to the end of largely unremarkable ones, so how did they all come to have the best years of their careers at precisely the same time? What was the particular combination of factors that came together simultaneously to make this team so good and so successful?

The Sum of the Parts is not just an account of what happened over those three incredible years. It's also an in-depth analysis of how and why it happened – from the very start of the process of putting this team together to their decline when all those factors were no longer present.

This isn't just a book for Reading supporters who want to celebrate such an incredible time in their club's history. It's a book for anyone interested in how football works or in discovering what the ingredients are which go together to make a team so much more than just a collection of players – one greater than the sum of its parts.

Lightning Source UK Ltd.
Milton Keynes UK
UKHW012339160620
365109UK00001B/135